DIAGRAM
COLLECTION

THE BEST IN
**GRAPHS, CHARTS,
MAPS,** AND
**TECHNICAL
ILLUSTRATION**

P·I·E BOOKS

DIAGRAM COLLECTION

P•I•E BOOKS

Villa Phoenix Suite 301 4-14-6 Komagome, Toshima-ku, Tokyo 170 Japan
Tel: 03-3940-8302 Fax: 03-3576-7361 e-mail: piebooks@bekkoame.or.jp

ISBN 4-89444-061-X C3070

First published in Germany 1997 by: **Nippan**
Nippon Shuppan Hanbai Deutschland GmbH Krefelder Strass 85,
D-40549 Düsseldorf , Germany Tel: 0211-5048080/89 Fax: 0211-5049326

ISBN 3-931884-06-6

Printed in Japan

本書は好評につき完売した「ダイアグラム グラフィックス」の改訂版です。
This book was previously published in a popular
hardcover edition as "DIAGRAM GRAPHICS".

P•I•E Books wishes to extend thanks to the following design firms
for allowing us to use their work on this book jacket.
Grundy & Northedge, Joel Katz Design Asscs, Pencil Corporate Art,
Pentagram Design / London, Pentagram Design / San Francisco,
Tatham Pearce Ltd., The Graphic Expression, Inc.

CONTENTS

4
FOREWORD

9
**STATISTICAL
TABLES & GRAPHS**

73
CHARTS & SCORES

121
MAPS

161
**ARCHITECTURAL
PLANS & DRAWINGS**

181
**INSTRUCTIONAL DIAGRAMS
FOR PRODUCTS**

199
**SCIENTIFIC
ILLUSTRATIONS**

217
INDEX

DIAGRAM GRAPHICS

現在、私たちはきわめて多様なメディアの吐きだす膨大な量の情報に取り囲まれて生きている。

新聞雑誌に代表される活字メディアが提供する文字情報、ラジオ・テレビに代表される電波メディアが提供する映像情報と音声情報、そして、活字メディア未来形ともいうべきパソコン通信等の電子メディアを介して交換される言語情報、加えて、ビデオの普及で完全に一般家庭への浸透を果たした映画等の高品質の画像情報……等々。

ともかく膨大な量の情報が、おそろしく多様な表現手段によって、私たちのもとへ送られてくるのが今日である。

こうした日々の生活は、知らずのうちに、私たちの情報というものに接する態度自体を根本から変えてしまっている。私たちの情報に対する感受性そのものが、飛躍的に多様化してしまい、もはや、文字情報のみによるコミュニケーション手段や、音声情報のみによるコミュニケーション手段では、新鮮な感動を得ることも、強い影響力をこうむることもむずかしい状況になっているのである。

こうした高度情報化社会に特有の、情報に対する感受性の多様化は、当然、印刷および映像の分野におけるデザインのありかたにも大きな影響を及ぼすことになる。

文字だけ、絵だけでは、こちらの思うような関心を示してくれなくなった読者たちの目を引き、気を引くために、印刷メディア、映像メディアを問わず、今後ますますデザイン需要を増すのが、本書で取り上げたダイアグラムというものである。

ダイアグラムとは、図表、図解など、文字情報だけでは伝わりにくい内容を、図形的なデザイン処理の力を借りて行なうものの総称である。

手法から見ても主題から見てもそのジャンルは多岐にわたるが、本書では、とりあえず、収録作品を下記の通りに分類し紹介してある。

1. 表・グラフ：統計や比較のためにデータを視覚化したもの
2. チャート・スコア：ものごとの関係や流れを視覚化したもの
3. マップ：空間や地域を視覚化したもの
4. 建築プラン：建築設計、都市計画等のための図解全般
5. 製品イラストレーション：製品、商品を紹介するための図解全般
6. 科学イラストレーション：現象、知識を解説するための図解全般

各ジャンルのダイアグラムの特徴等については、各章の扉のガイダンスを参照して頂きたい。

ダイアグラムの語源は、ギリシア語で「作図されたもの、図形」をいう「diagramma」にある。

「線を引くこと、描くこと」を表わす動詞「graphein」に、「～を通して」という意味を持つ「dia」がついて、「diagraphein」で、図形を指すようになった。

一目してわかる通り、「graphein」は、グラフィックの語源でもあり、グラフィック・デザインの分野そのものが、視覚化的な素材を効果的に利用してコミュニケーション効率の増大をはかるという姿勢において、「diagraphein」すなわちダイアグラムをその基本精神としているのである。

先にも述べたように、高度情報化社会のなかで多様化する一方の人々の情報感受性に的確に訴求するためには、この図形化されコミュニケーションとしてのダイアグラムは、ますますその真価を発揮するであろうし、また、いよいよ本格化する国際化社会においても、各国言語の障壁を超えるデザイン手法としてのダイアグラムの可能性は、さらに強い関心の的になるに違いない。

多様化し国際化するコミュニケーション環境における視覚言語の未来像を探り、出版に広告に、より説得力に富んだコミュニケーション手段の導入を模索する読者のために、本書が一助になれば幸いである。

西岡文彦

 序 文

FOREWORD

Fumihiko Nishioka

DIAGRAM GRAPHICS

The origin of the word "diagram" is the Greek "diagramma" which simply means, "Something drawn." The prefix "dia" means "via" and was attached to the verb "graphein" which means, "To draw a line, to draw." Obviously, "graphein" is also the origin of the word graphic.

Today we are surrounded by a staggering amount of information. It pours into our lives through a variety of diverse channels including text information via the printed media such as newspapers and magazines, visual and sound information via the broadcast media such as radio and TV and information which comes in new formats via new channels, such as the data exchanged via electronic networks of personal computers. In addition, information in the form of high-quality motion pictures and video documentaries, etc., has penetrated into the homes of ordinary families.

In short, the amount of information coming in through the mix of media to which we are all exposed, is vast. Living within this flood of input has become a way of life for most of us and without realizing it we have entirely changed our attitude towards information. The basic structure of our receptivity toward information has itself been diversified. In this new state we are unlikely to be moved or inspired or strongly influenced by any communication which depends upon, for example, text information only or sound information only. This diversification of human sensory mechanisms, which is undoubtedly inherent to life in a highly advanced information society, naturally has important ramifications in design for print and other visual media.

We have chosen to feature diagrams in this book, in part because it is clear that they are going to be of increasing importance in the future of print and visual media. More and more, diagrams will be required to attract the attention of, to stimulate and hold the interest of readers who will show less and less inclination to embrace a message delivered in plain text.

The word diagram is a general term for that which uses graphic design as an expository tool to convey something which would be difficult to explain with text alone. There are any number of genres of graphical communication which might fall under the general heading of diagrams, as viewed from the perspective of methodology, theme, intention and so forth. For this book, they have been classified and showcased in the following manner:

1. Statistical Tables & Graphs: Visualize data for the purpose of statistical comparison.

2. Charts & Scores: Visualize the relationships among and the flow of elements.

3. Maps: Visualize space and regions.

4. Architectural Plans & Drawings: A range of illustrations for architectural design, city planning etc.

5. Instructional Diagrams for Products: A range of illustrations which introduce products.

6. Scientific Illustrations: A range of illustrations that explain phenomena and knowledge.

Refer to the guide at the head of each chapter for detailed descriptions of the characteristics of the diagrams in each genre.

We might say that the graphic design field as a whole has the same fundamental objective as does the making of any individual diagram. That is, it reflects the attempt to increase the efficiency of communication by the effective use of visual material.

As mentioned before, in the future, diagrams will play an even greater role in communication by accurately focusing on the information receptors of contemporary people. In the borderless world of modern communication methods, the potential for diagrams as a design technique which overcomes language barriers, looms ever larger.

Amid the diversification and internationalization of our rapidly changing communication environment, we stumble forward in our attempts, largely by trial and error, to bring about more persuasive means of communication in publishing and advertising. We hope that this book will in some way help the reader who is interested in the images of a visual language for the future, to understand this exciting and dynamic process.

6

Das Wort "Diagramm" leitet sich vom dem griechischen Wort "diagramma" ab, das "etwas Gezeichnetes" bedeutet und durch Voranstellen der Vorsilbe "dia" (entspricht "via") vor das Verb "graphein" entstand. "Graphein" heißt "zeichnen, eine Linie ziehen" und aus diesem Begriff hat sich auch unser Wort "Graphik" entwickelt.

Wir sind heutzutage von einer erstaunlichen Menge an Informationen umgeben. Sie durchdringen unser Leben über eine Vielzahl von Kanälen, sowohl als Textinformation über die Printmedien wie Zeitungen und Zeitschriften, als visuelle und akustische Information über die Funkmedien Radio und Fernsehen und auch in neuer Form, wie es mit Datenübertragung in Computer-Netzwerken möglich ist. Der Video-Berelch hat sich als zusätzlicher Informationskanal mit Unterhaltung und Dokumentation etabliert, der bis in die Wohnzimmer vordringt.

Kurz, wir stehen einer unermeßlichen Informationsflut gegenüber. Wir haben uns daran gewöhnt, mit diesem Überangebot zu leben und ohne es zu bemerken, haben wir unsere Einstellung zu Informationen selbst verändert. Die Grundstruktur unserer Aufnahmefähigkeit für Informationen ist modifiziert. In diesem neuen Stadlum ist es sehr unwahrscheinlich, daß wir durch Informationen bewegt, beeinflußt oder inspiriert werden, deren Kommunikationsfähigkeit zum Beispiel nur von Text oder nur von Ton abhängt. Diese Veränderung der Wahrnehmungsfähigkeit, die mit dem Leben in einer hochentwickelten Informationsgesellschaft zwangsläufig einhergeht, hat natürlich weitreichende Auswirkungen im Design für Print- und andere Medien.

Wir haben uns entschlossen, in diesem Buch Diagramme vorzustellen, da sie eine steigende Bedeutung für die Zukunft der Print-und visuellen Medien haben werden. In zunehmendem Maße werden Diagramme notwendig sein, um Aufmerksamkeit und Interesse eines Leser zu wecken und zu binden, der immer weniger geneigt sein wird, eine Nachricht zu erfassen, die nur mit Text kommunizieren kann.

"Diagramm" steht als allgemeine Bezeichnung für alle Gestaltungen, die sich graphischer Techniken als Werkzeug bedienen, um etwas zu vermitteln, was mit Text allein nur schwer zu erklären ist. Es gibt daher eine Reihe von Genres graphischer Kommunikation, die unter den Oberbegriff "Diagramm" fallen, unterteilt nach Gesichtspunkten von Methodlk, Thematik, Intention etc. In diesem Buch werden die folgenden Einteilungen vorgestelit:

1. Tabellen-Graphiken: Visualisieren Daten zum statistischen Vergleich.

2. Übersichten, Flußdiagramme: Visualisieren den Zusammenhang zwischen und den Fluß von Elementen.

3.Landkarten: Visualisieren Landschaftsräume und Regionen.

4. Architektur-Pläne: Eine Reihe von Illustrationen für Architektur-Entwürfe, Stadtplanung etc.

5. Produkt-Illustration: Eine Reihe von Illustrationen, die Produkte vorstellen.

6. Wissenschaftliche Illustrationen: Eine Reihe von Illustrationen, die Phänomene und Sachzusammenhänge erklären.

In der Einleitung zu jedem Kapiteln werden detailliert die Charakteristiken der Graphiken in ihrem Genre vorgestellt. Wir möchten noch bemerken, daß Graphik-Design generell dieselben fundamentalen Vorgaben aufweist, wie das Erstellen eines individuellen Diagramms, nämlich die Reflexion des Versuches, die Effizienz der Kommunikation durch effektiven Einsatz visueller Mittel zu verbessern.

Wie bereits erwähnt, werden Diagramme im Kommunikationssystem eine immer größere Rolle spielen, da sie präzise auf die Rezeptoren der Information ausgerichtet werden können. In der grenzenlosen Welt der modemen Kommunikationsmethoden wird das Potential von Diagrammen, die Sprachgrenzen problemlos überwinden können, immer bedeutungsvoller.

Inmitten der Diversifikation und Internationalisierung unserer rasch wechselnden kommunikativen Umgebung bemühen wir uns ständig, Kommunikationsmittel mit größerer Überzeugungskraft für die Publikation und Werbung zu entwickeln-oftmals mittels Versuch und Irrtum. Wir hoffen, daß dieses Buch dem an den Bildern einer zukünftigen visuellen Sprache interessierten Leser auf die eine oder andere Art hilft, diesen aufregenden und faszinierenden Vorgang zu verstehen.

Fumihiko Nishioka

VORWORT

また、国名の表示に関しては出品者の居住国を表記しています。

作品説明は出品者より送られたものを記載し、それ以外のものについては小社で作成しました。

EDITORIAL NOTE:

CD: Creative Director

AD: Art Director

D: Designer

P: Photographer

I: Illustrator

PR: Producer

DF: Design Firm

クレジットのタイトルに関しては、クライアント名を
また、国名の表示に関しては出品者の居住国を表記しています。
作品説明は出品者より送られたものを記載し、それ以外のものについては小社で作成しました。

The title of each credit indicates the name of the commissioning client.
The country indicated for each entry is the country in which the artist resides.
Most of the descriptions accompanying the diagrams
in this book have been reproduced as received from the artists themselves.
The others were prepared by the Editorial Department of P·I·E Books.

DIAGRAM GRAPHICS

STATISTICAL
TABLES & GRAPHS

データは整理されていなければ、単なる情報の寄せ集めである。ここで紹介する表とグラフは、データを整理、分類し、一定の法則に従って図形的に配置し、視覚的に変換したダイアグラムのことをいう。

表は、普通、タテ軸とヨコ軸の二系列にそれぞれ別の項目を設定し、データを配置する形式をとる。整理、分類されたデータを体系的に配列し、データ相互の対応関係を確認するためのダイアグラムであり、グラフをはじめとする他のダイアグラムを作成するための基本となる作業でもある。

作成にあたっては、データの読み取りやすい明快な構成を心がけたい。線と文字による表組みは、ともすれば単調な画面となりやすいだけに、デザイン上の工夫が求められる。ただし、データの読み取りやすさをそこなっては、本来の表の機能が果たせないので、タイポグラフィにせよ、色彩設計にせよ、表本来の明確な性格を損なわない抑制した処置が望まれる。

グラフは、単に、データを整理、分類するのではなく、一定の法則に従って視覚的に変換されたものを配置したダイアグラムのことをいう。

数字を線に変換すれば線グラフ、面に変換すれば面グラフというように、データを視覚的な「量」に置き換えることで、具体的な比較を容易にするためのダイアグラムである。グラフの特徴は、抽象的な情報を具体的な形に変換して、明確なイメージとして提示し、データを直観的に把握し比較できるようにする点にある。

したがって、グラフの制作にあたっては、棒グラフのようにデータを線の長さに置き換えるのか、円グラフのように面の広さに置き換えて、量を比較するのか、あるいは折れ線グラフのように点を結んだ線として示し、データの量の変化を示すか、データの性格とグラフの目的にかなった視覚的要素の、的確な選定がカギとなる。

単なる棒の代わりに鉛筆を使ったり、単なる面の代わりに具体的な地図を使ったりして、ややもすれば統計的、数学的な冷たい表情を示しやすいグラフに、よりソフトな表情を加えることも大切な工夫である。

表 & グラフ

Data which have not been sorted and classified are merely a chaotic hodgepodge of raw information. The tables and graphs introduced here are examples of the type of diagrams in which data are sorted and classified and then laid-out according to certain graphical rules to form a visual presentation.

Normally, such a diagram basically takes the form of intersecting vertical and horizontal axes, whereupon the separate items are set out on the respective scales; the *rank* and *file*, or the *x* axis and *y* axis. It is a diagram for arranging sorted and classified data systematically and for verifying the corresponding relationships among different sets of data. A table can be a finished presentation, or it might be a preparatory arrangement of data that serves as a basis for a graph or some other kind of diagram.

In creating a table, one should bear in mind that it should have a clear structure that facilitates reading the data. The composition of a table featuring lines and text tends to be somewhat monotonous and that is why you have to be as innovative as possible. However, if, because of your designer's contrivances, you detract from the readability of the data, then the table will fail in its original function. In terms of general design, choice of typefaces, overall color scheme and so forth, a degree of restraint must be exercised so that the diagram will not lose its essential characteristic; that of a precision visual instrument for conveying information.

A graph, then, is a diagram in which data are not simply sorted and classified but also converted to a visual form in accordance with certain pictorial rules. If a set of numbers is converted to lines, for example, this will constitute a line graph, if converted to areas, then perhaps, a pie graph. The purpose of this sort of diagram, of course, is to make it easier to compare data by converting it into a clear visual form which represents quantitative information.

One of the main characteristics of a graph is that it offers easy and direct visual understanding and comparison of abstract numerical data. Once converted to simple shapes and forms, a definite and clear image of the meaning of the data becomes apparent. When producing graphs, therefore, the key is to choose the visual elements carefully so that they will be appropriate to the nature of the data you are working with. If your terms are expressed in percentages, for example, a pie graph might be the most accessible way of presenting it. On the other hand, if you want to demonstrate they way your values have changed over time, a polygonal line graph might work best.

It is of the utmost importance, in any case, that a graph be rendered in a viewer-friendly format. One effective design choice is to employ familiar representative objects as the main visual elements; pencils instead of bars, for example, or maps instead of featureless areas. Without this sort of effort, a graph will tend to wear a rather cold statistical image and will remain unappealing.

STATISTICAL TABLES & GRAPHS

表 & グラフ

AMERICAN PACIFIC CORPORATION
USA 1991
CD:Thomas Page
AD:Don Kano
D,I:Faith Ishibashi
DF:Kano Design Group

CHARTS & SCORES

MAPS

ARCHITECTURAL
PLANS & DRAWINGS

INSTRUCTIONAL DIAGRAMS
FOR PRODUCTS

SCIENTIFIC
ILLUSTRATIONS

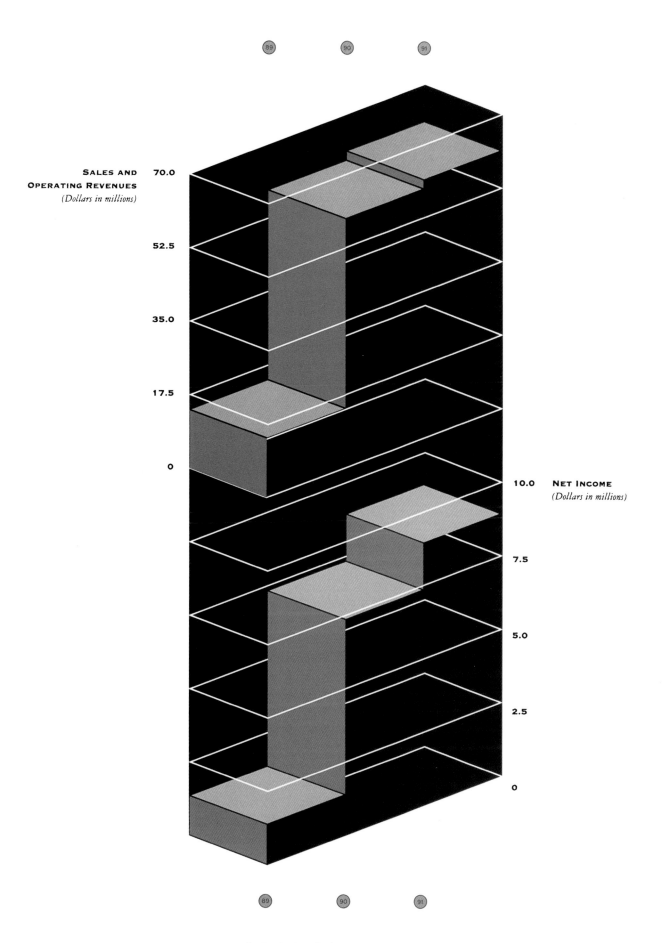

Graphs showing sales & operating revenues and net income.
The grid lines in these graphs create an environment as well as a strong sense of structure. From an American Pacific Corporation annual report.
アメリカン・パシフィック社のアニュアルリポートより、販売や営業による収益と純利益を表したグラフ。グラフ中の格子線は正確かつ印象的なデザイン表現のポイントとなっている。

STATISTICAL
TABLES & GRAPHS

CHARTS & SCORES

MAPS

ARCHITECTURAL
PLANS & DRAWINGS

INSTRUCTIONAL DIAGRAMS
FOR PRODUCTS

SCIENTIFIC
ILLUSTRATIONS

CLABIR CORPORATION
USA 1983
CD:Jack Hough
AD,D:Tom Morin
I:Jerry Hablitzel
DF:Jack Hough Associates, Inc.

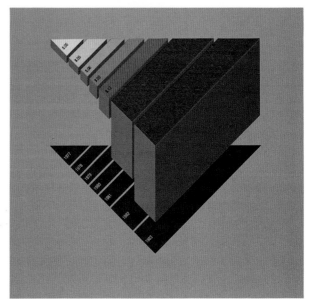

Graphs highlighting Clabir Corporation's financial success over the previous decade. From a corporate annual report.
クラビル社のアニュアルリポートより、同社の過去10年間の財政上の成功に焦点を当てたグラフ。

STATISTICAL
TABLES & GRAPHS

CHARTS & SCORES

MAPS

ARCHITECTURAL
PLANS & DRAWINGS

INSTRUCTIONAL DIAGRAMS
FOR PRODUCTS

SCIENTIFICAL
ILLUSTRATIONS

GENERAL DEFENSE CORPORATION
USA 1984
CD,AD:Jack Hough
D:Henry Goerke
P:Jerry Sarpochiello
I:Nick Fasciano
DF:Jack Hough Associates, Inc.

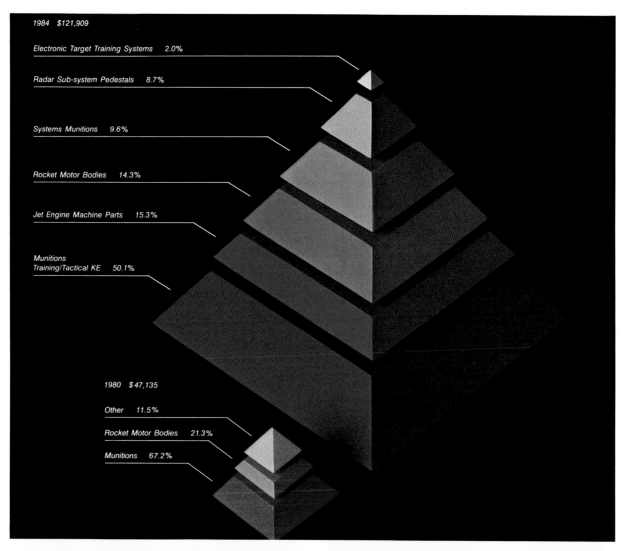

1984 $121,909

Electronic Target Training Systems   2.0%

Radar Sub-system Pedestals   8.7%

Systems Munitions   9.6%

Rocket Motor Bodies   14.3%

Jet Engine Machine Parts   15.3%

Munitions
Training/Tactical KE   50.1%

1980 $47,135

Other   11.5%

Rocket Motor Bodies   21.3%

Munitions   67.2%

These financial graphs were constructed out of plastic, painted and displayed as full-page illustrations. From a General Defense Corporation annual report.
ジェネラル・ディフェンス社のアニュアルリポートより、プラスチック素材を使用してページいっぱいに表現した財務に関するグラフ。

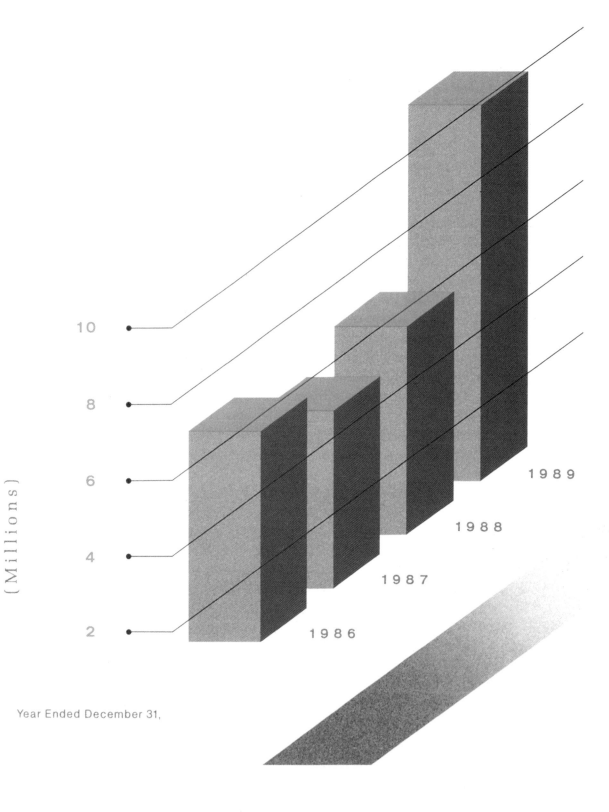

STATISTICAL
TABLES & GRAPHS

CHARTS & SCORES

MAPS

ARCHITECTURAL
PLANS & DRAWINGS

INSTRUCTIONAL DIAGRAMS
FOR PRODUCTS

SCIENTIFIC
ILLUSTRATIONS

(Millions)

10

8

6

4

2

1986

1987

1988

1989

Year Ended December 31,

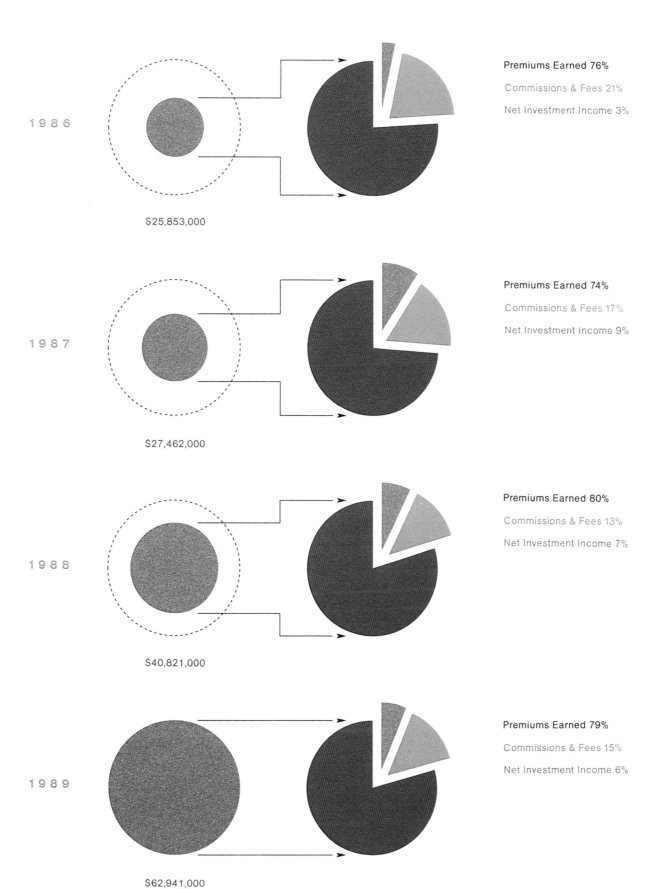

TOTAL REVENUE   BY SOURCE

STATISTICAL TABLES & GRAPHS

CHARTS & SCORES

MAPS

ARCHITECTURAL PLANS & DRAWINGS

INSTRUCTIONAL DIAGRAMS FOR PRODUCTS

SCIENTIFIC ILLUSTRATIONS

1986

$25,853,000

Premiums Earned 76%

Commissions & Fees 21%

Net Investment Income 3%

1987

$27,462,000

Premiums Earned 74%

Commissions & Fees 17%

Net Investment Income 9%

1988

$40,821,000

Premiums Earned 80%

Commissions & Fees 13%

Net Investment Income 7%

1989

$62,941,000

Premiums Earned 79%

Commissions & Fees 15%

Net Investment Income 6%

Three-dimensional bar graph appears to hover over a drop shadow that represents the base line.
Graphs showing the growth in revenues while demonstrating the composition of revenues by source. From a U.S. Facilities Corp. annual report.
USファシリティーズ社のアニュアルリポートより、ベースラインを影で表し、その上に浮かせるデザインを採用した立体棒グラフ、及び資金源と対比して表した歳入のグラフ。

STATISTICAL
TABLES & GRAPHS

CHARTS & SCORES

MAPS

ARCHITECTURAL
PLANS & DRAWINGS

INSTRUCTIONAL DIAGRAMS
FOR PRODUCTS

SCIENTIFIC
ILLUSTRATIONS

U.S. FACILITIES CORPORATION
USA 1990
CD,AD:Don Kano
D:Mike Mescall
DF:Kano Design Group

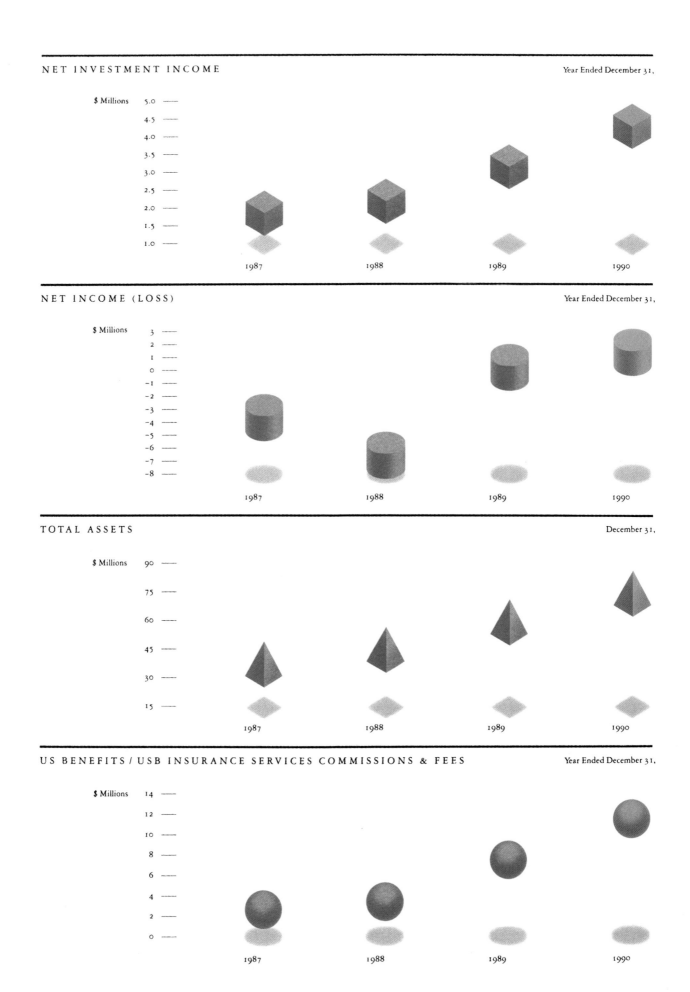

NET INVESTMENT INCOME   Year Ended December 31,

NET INCOME (LOSS)   Year Ended December 31,

TOTAL ASSETS   December 31,

US BENEFITS / USB INSURANCE SERVICES COMMISSIONS & FEES   Year Ended December 31,

Percent   Years 1970–1988

COMPARISON OF GROWTH RATES OF GNP AND NATIONAL HEALTH EXPENDITURES

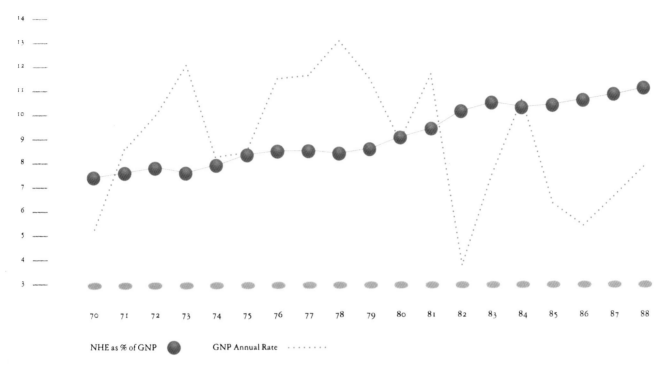

NHE as % of GNP ●   GNP Annual Rate · · · · · · · ·

Sources: U.S. Department of Health and Human Services, Health Care Financing Administration, Health Care Financing Notes, July 1989 and unpublished data from the U.S. Department of Commerce.

TOTAL REVENUES

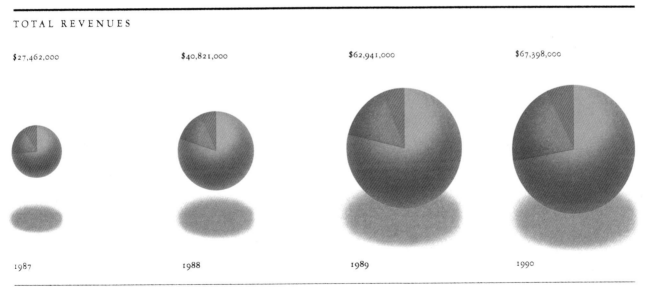

$27,462,000 $40,821,000 $62,941,000 $67,398,000

1987   1988   1989   1990

BY SOURCE

Premiums Earned 74%	Premiums Earned 80%	Premiums Earned 79%	Premiums Earned 73%
Commissions & Fees 17%	Commissions & Fees 13%	Commissions & Fees 15%	Commissions & Fees 20%
Net Investment Income 9%	Net Investment Income 7%	Net Investment Income 6%	Net Investment Income 7%

The basic geometry of the cube, sphere, pyramid and cylinder was employed as a simple but effective way to satisfy a wide range of chart requirements including bar graphs, a mountain graph and pie graphs. From a U.S. Facilities Corp. annual report.

USファシリティーズ社のアニュアルリポートより、より印象的な表現のために立方体・球・三角錐・円筒などを利用した棒グラフ、山型グラフ、円グラフ。

NYNEX CORPORATION
USA 1991
CD:Meera Singh
AD:Lynn Martin
D:Jennifer Choi
DF:Inc Design

ナイネックス社のアニュアルリポートより、財務に関するグラフ。

Fiscal graphs from a Nynex Corporation annual report.
ナイネックス社のアニュアルリポートより、財務に関するグラフ。

STATISTICAL
TABLES & GRAPHS

CHARTS & SCORES

MAPS

ARCHITECTURAL
PLANS & DRAWINGS

INSTRUCTIONAL DIAGRAMS
FOR PRODUCTS

SCIENTIFIC
ILLUSTRATIONS

BANPONCE CORPORATION
USA 1990
AD:Howard Belk
D:Carin Benger
I:In House
DF:Belk Mignogna Associates Ltd.

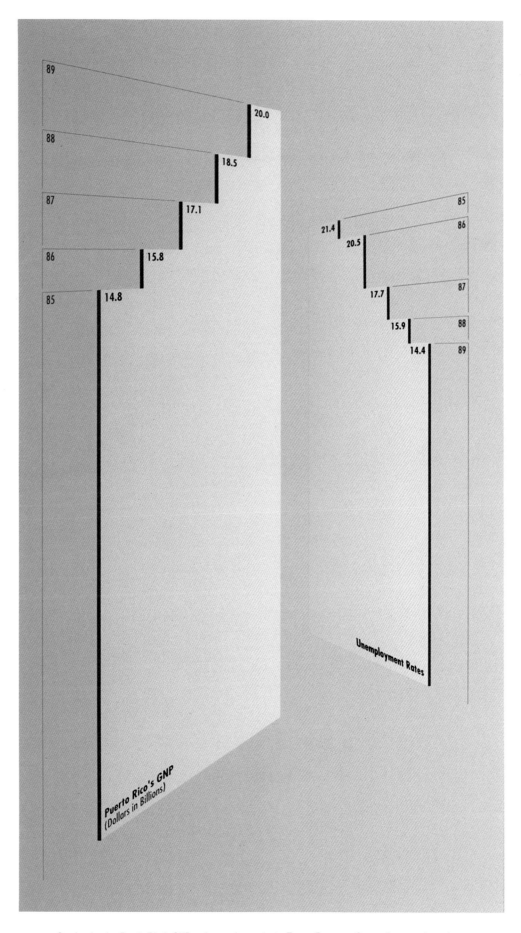

Graphs showing Puerto Rico's GNP and unemployment rate. From a Banponce Corporation annual report.
バンポンス社のアニュアルリポートより、プエルトリコのGNP、及び失業率を表したチャート。

STATISTICAL
TABLES & GRAPHS

CHARTS & SCORES

MAPS

ARCHITECTURAL
PLANS & DRAWINGS

INSTRUCTIONAL DIAGRAMS
FOR PRODUCTS

SCIENTIFIC
ILLUSTRATIONS

GOLD PEAK
INDUSTRIES(HOLDINGS)LIMITED
HONG KONG 1990,1991
CD,AD:Kan Tai-Keung
AD,D:Eddy Yu Chi Kong
DF:Kan Tai-Keung Design & Associates Ltd.

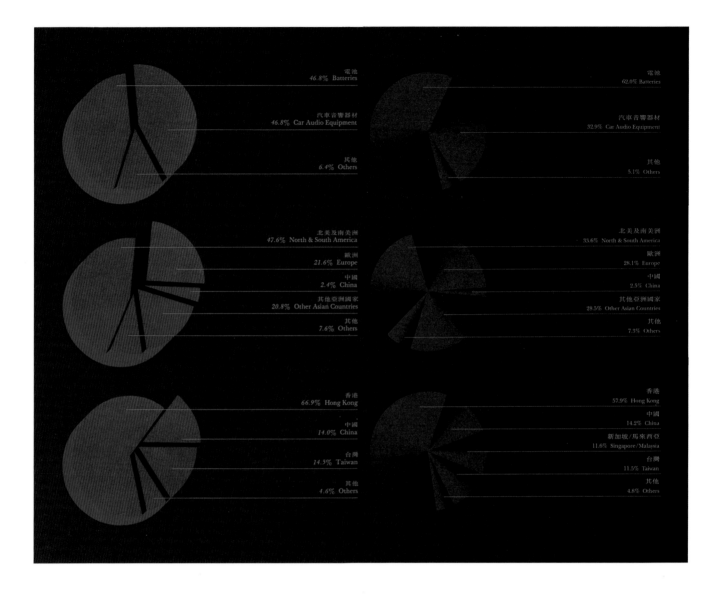

電池
46.8% Batteries

汽車音響器材
46.8% Car Audio Equipment

其他
6.4% Others

電池
62.0% Batteries

汽車音響器材
32.9% Car Audio Equipment

其他
5.1% Others

北美及南美洲
47.6% North & South America

歐洲
21.6% Europe

中國
2.4% China

其他亞洲國家
20.8% Other Asian Countries

其他
7.6% Others

北美及南美洲
33.6% North & South America

歐洲
28.1% Europe

中國
2.5% China

其他亞洲國家
28.5% Other Asian Countries

其他
7.3% Others

香港
66.9% Hong Kong

中國
14.0% China

台灣
14.5% Taiwan

其他
4.6% Others

香港
57.9% Hong Kong

中國
14.2% China

新加坡/馬來西亞
11.6% Singapore/Malaysia

台灣
11.5% Taiwan

其他
4.8% Others

Financial graphs from a Gold Peak Industries Ltd. annual report.
ゴールドピーク・インダストリーズ社のアニュアルリポートより、財務に関するグラフ。

STATISTICAL
TABLES & GRAPHS

CHARTS & SCORES

MAPS

ARCHITECTURAL
PLANS & DRAWINGS

INSTRUCTIONAL DIAGRAMS
FOR PRODUCTS

SCIENTIFIC
ILLUSTRATIONS

1. SEIYU CO., LTD.
JAPAN 1982
CD,AD,D:Tetsuya Ohta

**2. THE SEIBU GROUP OF
RETAIL ENTERPRISES**
JAPAN 1985
CD,AD,D:Tetsuya Ohta

1

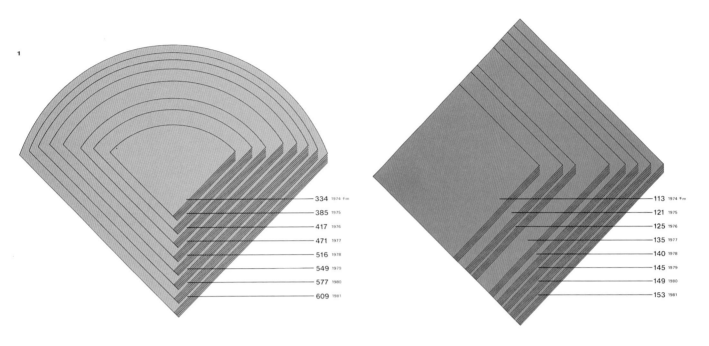

334 1974 ㎡	113 1974 ㎡
385 1975	121 1975
417 1976	125 1976
471 1977	135 1977
516 1978	140 1978
549 1979	145 1979
577 1980	149 1980
609 1981	153 1981

2

18,493,410
18,434,914
18,397,132

11,387,848
11,356,041

1980 1981 1982 1983 1984

1. Annual changes of sales floor area of the supermarket chain, Seiyu.
スーパーマーケット「西友」の年間売場面積推移図。

2. Changes in the land area developed by the real estate
department of Seibu Group of Retail Enterprises.
西武流通グループ/不動産部門の開発面積推移図。

STATISTICAL TABLES & GRAPHS

CHARTS & SCORES

MAPS

ARCHITECTURAL PLANS & DRAWINGS

INSTRUCTIONAL DIAGRAMS FOR PRODUCTS

SCIENTIFIC ILLUSTRATIONS

CIRCUS CIRCUS ENTERPRISES, INC.

USA 1989

CD,AD,D:Don Kano

I:Carlos Delgado

DF:Kano Design Group

LONG ISLAND SAVINGS BANK

USA 1988

AD,D:Georgna Leaf

DF:Lintas Marketing Communications

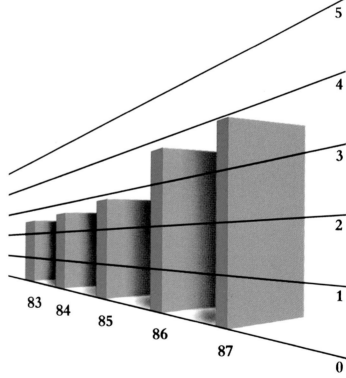

An alternative to the traditional pie chart.
There are 100 cubes in each graph with each cube representing one percent of the total.
From a Circus Circus Enterprises, Inc. annual report.
サーカス・サーカス・エンタープライズ社のアニュアルリポートより、
一般的に使用される円グラフに代わって100個のキューブを採用したグラフ。1個のキューブが1パーセントを表す。

Fiscal graphs from a Long Island Savings Bank annual report.
ロングアイランド貯蓄銀行のアニュアルリポートより、財務報告のためのグラフ。

STATISTICAL
TABLES & GRAPHS

CHARTS & SCORES

MAPS

ARCHITECTURAL
PLANS & DRAWINGS

INSTRUCTIONAL DIAGRAMS
FOR PRODUCTS

SCIENTIFIC
ILLUSTRATIONS

**CHAMPION INTERNATIONAL
CORPORATION**
USA 1985
CD:Jack Hough
AD,D:Tom Morin
I:Paul Giovanopoulos
DF:Jack Hough Associates, Inc.

LOCKHEED CORPORATION
USA 1990
CD,AD,D:Carl Seltzer
DF:Carl Seltzer Design Office

The Champion International annual report focused primarily
on the company's financial results. To make the report more interesting,
an artist was commissioned to draw the graphs with colored pencils.
チャンピオン・インターナショナル社のアニュアルリポートより、
色鉛筆を使用することでより印象を高めている財務関連のグラフ。

In these fiscal graphs, subtle but distinctive colors were
chosen to make each section of the bar clear.
From a Lockheed Corporation annual report.
ロッキード社のアニュアルリポートより、各棒の配色が微妙でありながら、
はっきりと判別できるよう工夫された財務関連のグラフ。

STATISTICAL
TABLES & GRAPHS

CHARTS & SCORES

MAPS

ARCHITECTURAL
PLANS & DRAWINGS

INSTRUCTIONAL DIAGRAMS
FOR PRODUCTS

SCIENTIFIC
ILLUSTRATIONS

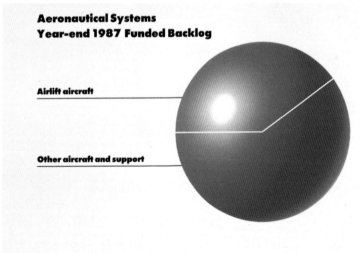

Graphs illustrating corporate operating state. From a Lockheed Corporation annual report.
ロッキード社のアニュアルリポートより、同社の経営状況に関するグラフ。

MOUNTAIN BELL
(U.S. WEST COMMUNICATIONS)
USA 1985
CD,AD,D:Errol Beauchamp
P:Paul Peregrine
I:Martin Miller
DF:Beauchamp Group/Denver

CHARTS & SCORES

MAPS

ARCHITECTURAL
PLANS & DRAWINGS

INSTRUCTIONAL DIAGRAMS
FOR PRODUCTS

SCIENTIFIC
ILLUSTRATIONS

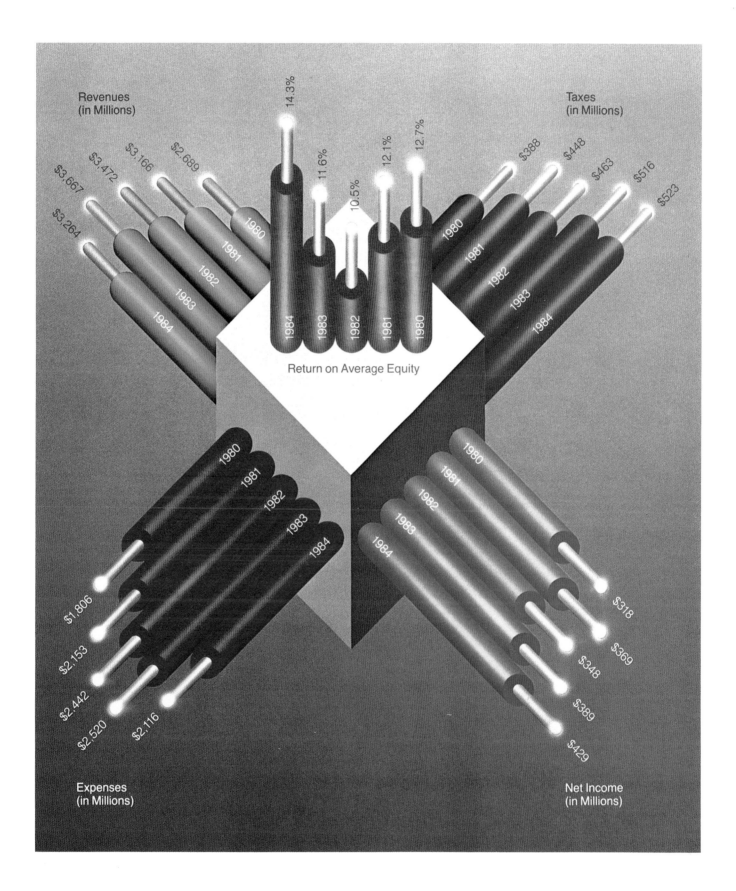

Diagram of selected financial data using fiber optic cable technology as the primary picture element. From a Mountain Bell annual report.
マウンテン・ベル社のアニュアルリポートより、光ファイバーケーブルをモチーフにして財務データを表したグラフ。

**STATISTICAL
TABLES & GRAPHS**

CHARTS & SCORES

MAPS

ARCHITECTURAL
PLANS & DRAWINGS

INSTRUCTIONAL DIAGRAMS
FOR PRODUCTS

SCIENTIFIC
ILLUSTRATIONS

ROCHE PRODUCTS LIMITED
ENGLAND 1971
CD,AD,D:Mervyn Kurlansky
D:Maddy Bennet
DF:Pentagram Design Ltd.

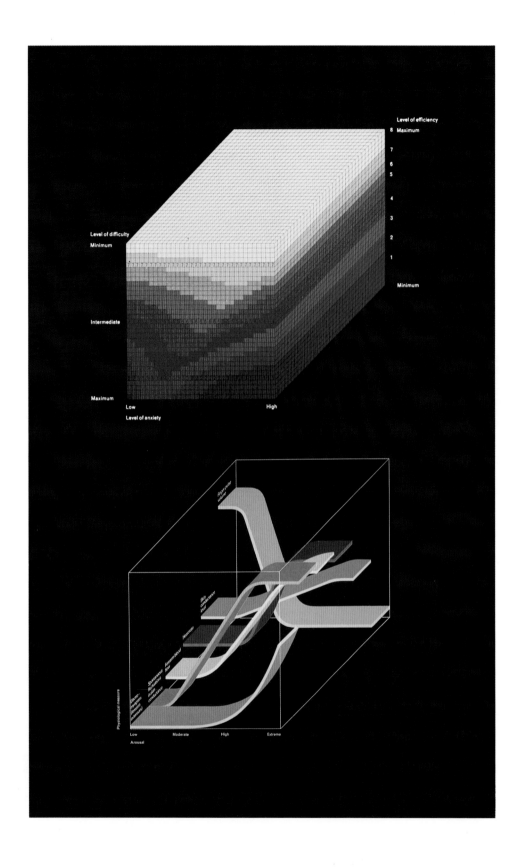

Illustration showing the effect anxiety has on the efficiency with which tasks are carried out.
From a Roche Products Limited promotional brochure for a new tranquillizer.
ロッシュ・プロダクツ社の新精神安定剤プロモーション用パンフレットより、
不安が遂行中の仕事に及ぼす影響を示すグラフ。

A physical profile of anxiety
- steepness of the curve indicates the speed of change taking place.
心理的不安が肉体に及ぼす影響のグラフ。曲線の傾斜が変化の速度を示している。

STATISTICAL
TABLES & GRAPHS

CHARTS & SCORES

MAPS

ARCHITECTURAL
PLANS & DRAWINGS

INSTRUCTIONAL DIAGRAMS
FOR PRODUCTS

SCIENTIFIC
ILLUSTRATIONS

FEDERAL EXPRESS CORPORATION
USA 1989
CD:Stephen Ferrari
I:Javier Romero
DF:The Graphic Expression, Inc.

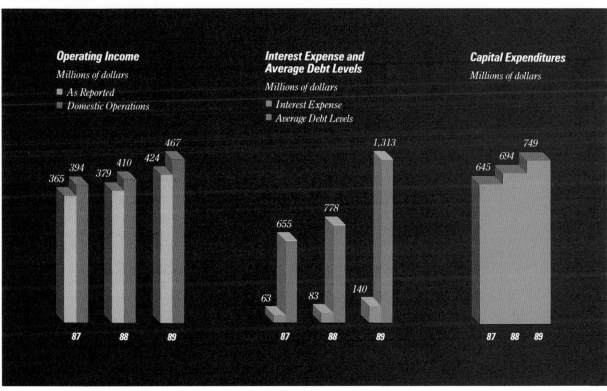

Graphs visualizing important financial measures which accompanied the management discussion and analysis of operating results.
From a Federal Express Corporation annual report.
フェデラル・エクスプレス社のアニュアルリポートより、経営論議や運営結果の分析にともなった重要な財政方策を視覚化するチャート。

STATISTICAL
TABLES & GRAPHS

CHARTS & SCORES

MAPS

ARCHITECTURAL
PLANS & DRAWINGS

INSTRUCTIONAL DIAGRAMS
FOR PRODUCTS

SCIENTIFIC
ILLUSTRATIONS

Annual changes in the performance of the supermarket chain, Seiyu.
スーパーマーケット「西友」の年間業績推移図。

STATISTICAL
TABLES & GRAPHS

CHARTS & SCORES

MAPS

ARCHITECTURAL
PLANS & DRAWINGS

INSTRUCTIONAL DIAGRAMS
FOR PRODUCTS

SCIENTIFIC
ILLUSTRATIONS

BOSTON UNIVERSITY MEDICAL CENTER
USA 1991
CD,D:Michael McPherson
I:Fred Lynch
DF:Corey McPherson Nash

HARVARD LAW SCHOOL
USA 1990
CD,AD,D:Michael McPherson
DF:Corey McPherson Nash

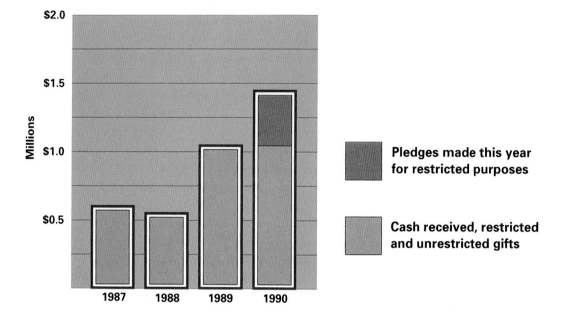

**Pledges made this year
for restricted purposes**

**Cash received, restricted
and unrestricted gifts**

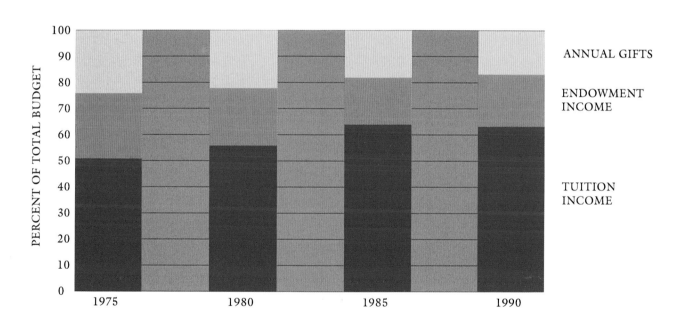

ANNUAL GIFTS

ENDOWMENT
INCOME

TUITION
INCOME

Graph of fund raising achievement.
From a Boston University Medical Center annual report.
ボストン大学医療センターのアニュアルリポートより、基金開発の成功を示すグラフ。

Graph of annual gifts and endowment income.
From a Harvard Law School promotional brochure.
ハーバード・ロウ・スクールのプロモーション用パンフレットより、年間の寄贈収益のグラフ。

STATISTICAL
TABLES & GRAPHS

CHARTS & SCORES

MAPS

ARCHITECTURAL
PLANS & DRAWINGS

INSTRUCTIONAL DIAGRAMS
FOR PRODUCTS

SCIENTIFIC
ILLUSTRATIONS

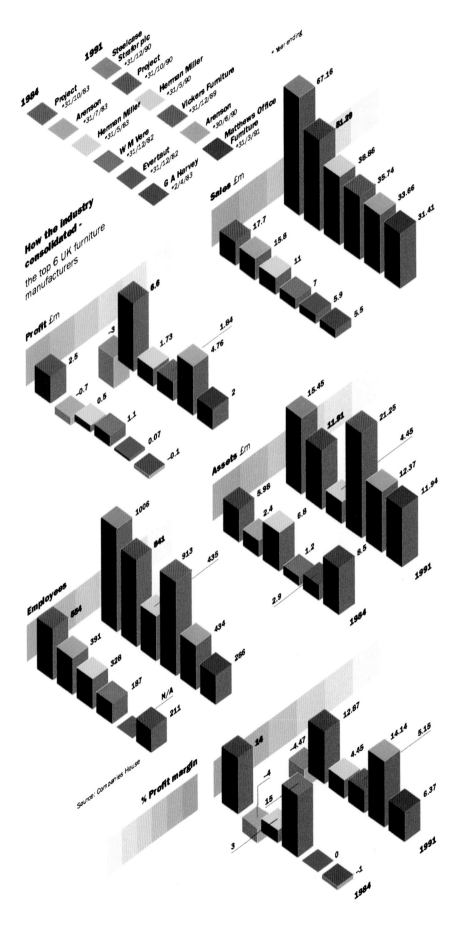

Graph of the top 6 UK furniture manufacturers showing how the industry consolidated. From Design magazine.
「デザインマガジン」より、英国の家具産業がいかに整理統合されてきたかを示す上位６社のグラフ。

STATISTICAL
TABLES & GRAPHS

CHARTS & SCORES

MAPS

ARCHITECTURAL
PLANS & DRAWINGS

INSTRUCTIONAL DIAGRAMS
FOR PRODUCTS

SCIENTIFIC
ILLUSTRATIONS

FORBES MAGAZINE
USA 1992
AD:Everett Halvorsen
D,I:Andy Christie

CENTOCOR, INC.
USA 1990
CD:Charles C. Cabot III
AD,D:Joel Katz
I:Stacey Lewis
DF:Katz Wheeler Design

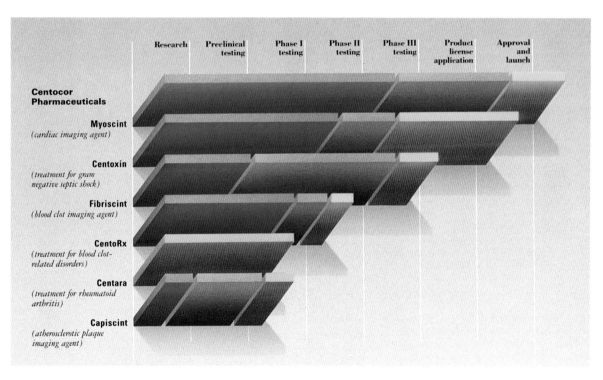

Graphs showing the GNP and GDP of various countries.
From an article on the present economic situation in Canada, in Forbes magazine.
「フォーブスマガジン」より、"カナダ経済の現況"の記事に使用された各国のGNPとGDPを表すグラフ。

Phase diagram showing the progressive development of pharmaceutical products.
From a Centocor, Inc. annual report.
セントコア社のアニュアルリポートより、医薬品の製造過程を示す段階図。

S T A T I S T I C A L
TABLES & GRAPHS

CHARTS & SCORES

MAPS

ARCHITECTURAL
PLANS & DRAWINGS

INSTRUCTIONAL DIAGRAMS
FOR PRODUCTS

SCIENTIFIC
ILLUSTRATIONS

1. BOSTON UNIVERSITY
MEDICAL CENTER
USA 1992
CD,AD,D:Michael McPherson
DF:Corey McPherson Nash

2. UNOCAL CORPORATION
USA 1986
CD,AD,I:Ray Engle
D,I:Debra Hampton
DF:Ray Engle & Associates

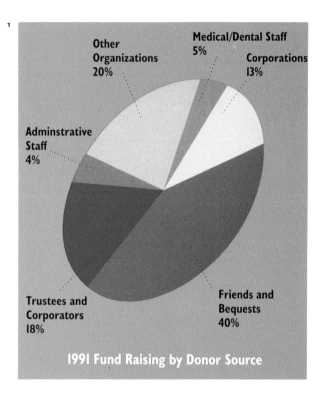

Other
Organizations
20%

Medical/Dental Staff
5%

Corporations
13%

Adminstrative
Staff
4%

Trustees and
Corporators
18%

Friends and
Bequests
40%

1991 Fund Raising by Donor Source

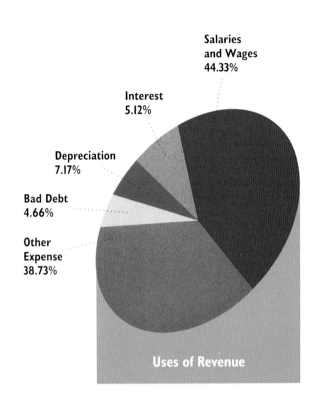

Salaries
and Wages
44.33%

Interest
5.12%

Depreciation
7.17%

Bad Debt
4.66%

Other
Expense
38.73%

Uses of Revenue

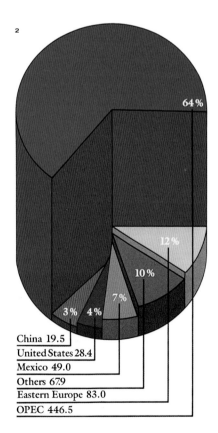

64%

12%

10%

7%

3%   4%

China 19.5
United States 28.4
Mexico 49.0
Others 67.9
Eastern Europe 83.0
OPEC 446.5

1. Graphs of 1991 Funds by Donor Source and Uses of Revenue.
From a Boston University Medical Center annual report.
ボストン大学医療センターのアニュアルリポートより、
1991年度基金源、及び歳入の使途についてのグラフ。

2. Graph showing estimated world crude oil reserves.
From a magazine article on America's energy future.
"アメリカのエネルギー事情の今後"についての雑誌記事より、
全世界の原油推定埋蔵量を表すグラフ。

STATISTICAL TABLES & GRAPHS

CHARTS & SCORES

MAPS

ARCHITECTURAL PLANS & DRAWINGS

INSTRUCTIONAL DIAGRAMS FOR PRODUCTS

SCIENTIFIC ILLUSTRATIONS

1. HARVARD LAW SCHOOL
USA 1990
CD,AD,D:Michael McPherson
DF:Corey McPherson Nash

2. FREMONT GENERAL CORPORATION
USA 1991
CD,AD,D:Carl Seltzer
D:Chris Wevers
DF:Carl Seltzer Design Office

3. GREAT WESTERN FINANCIAL CORPORATION
USA 1992
CD,AD,D:Carl Seltzer
D:Luis Alvarado
DF:Carl Seltzer Design Office

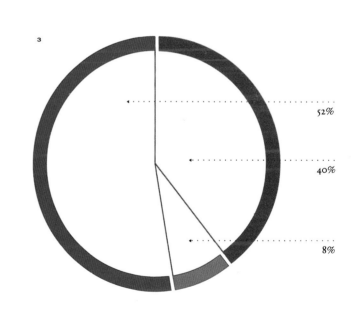

1. Graph of Income
from a Harvard Law School promotional brochure.
ハーバード・ロウ・スクールの
プロモーション用パンフレットより、収益のグラフ。

2. Graph clearly showing the company's percentage of the California market in worker's compensation insurance. From a Fremont General Corporation annual report.
フリーモント・ジェネラル社のアニュアルリポートより、
勤労者保証保険のカリフォルニア・マーケットにおける
同社の占める割合を示したグラフ。

3. Graph showing new adjustment rate mortgages. The bright colors and legible type add to the overall 'upbeat' feeling. From a Great Western Financial Corporation annual report.
グレートウエスタン・ファイナンシャル社の
アニュアルリポートより、明るい配色で軽快に表現された
新調整金利抵当に関するグラフ。

**GREAT WESTERN FINANCIAL
CORPORATION**
USA 1991
CD,AD,D:Carl Seltzer
DF:Carl Seltzer Design Office

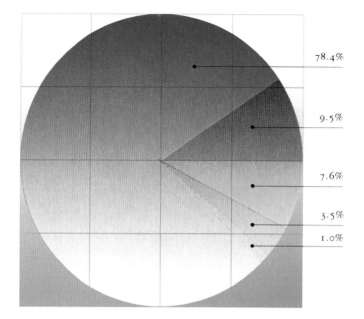

78.4%

9.5%

7.6%

3.5%

1.0%

These bar, pie, line and mountain financial graphs were all designed to work together with subtle gradations in both the backgrounds and foregrounds.
From a Great Western Financial Corporation annual report.
グレートウエスタン・ファイナンシャル社のアニュアルリポートより、デザインに微妙なグラデーションを採用し、印象的に表現された財務関連のグラフ。

STATISTICAL
TABLES &
GRAPHS

CHARTS & SCORES

MAPS

ARCHITECTURAL
PLANS & DRAWINGS

INSTRUCTIONAL DIAGRAMS
FOR PRODUCTS

SCIENTIFIC
ILLUSTRATIONS

STAR PAGING
(INTERNATIONAL HOLDING)LIMITED
HONG KONG 1992
CD,AD:Kan Tai-Keung
AD:Clement Yick Tat Wa
D:Janny Lee Yin Wa
DF:Kan Tai-Keung Design & Associates Ltd.

THE WCRS GROUP PLC
ENGLAND
AD:Amanda Tatham
D,I:Gill Davies
DF:Tatham Pearce Ltd.

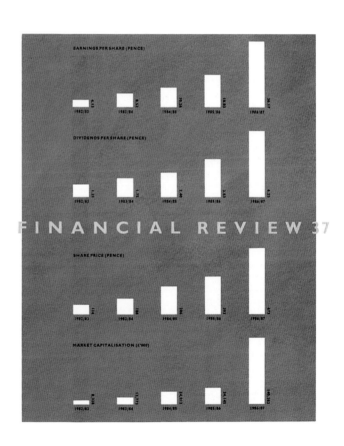

Graph showing the number of subscribers. From Star Paging Ltd. annual report.
スター・ページング社のアニュアルリポートより、労働者数を表したグラフ。

Financial review from the WCRS Group's annual report.
WCRSグループのアニュアルリポートより、財務評論のためのグラフ。

STATISTICAL
TABLES & GRAPHS

CHARTS & SCORES

MAPS

ARCHITECTURAL
PLANS & DRAWINGS

INSTRUCTIONAL DIAGRAMS
FOR PRODUCTS

SCIENTIFIC
ILLUSTRATIONS

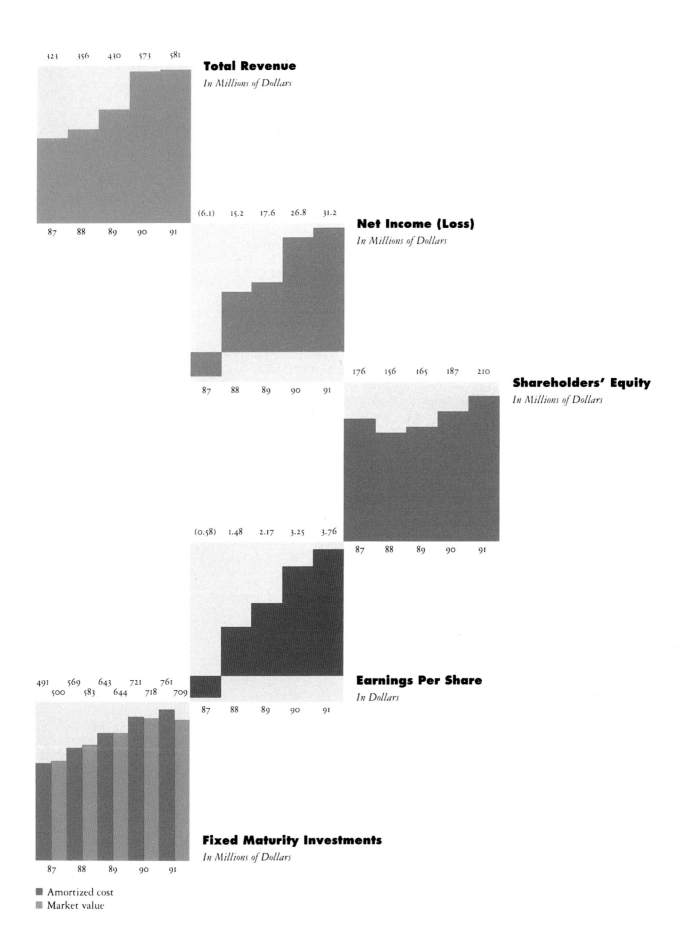

Total Revenue
In Millions of Dollars

323　356　430　573　581

87　88　89　90　91

Net Income (Loss)
In Millions of Dollars

(6.1)　15.2　17.6　26.8　31.2

87　88　89　90　91

Shareholders' Equity
In Millions of Dollars

176　156　165　187　210

87　88　89　90　91

Earnings Per Share
In Dollars

(0.58)　1.48　2.17　3.25　3.76

87　88　89　90　91

Fixed Maturity Investments
In Millions of Dollars

491　569　643　721　761
　500　583　644　718　709

87　88　89　90　91

■ Amortized cost
■ Market value

The design and colors used in these graphs are coordinated with the photos and other elements in the report. From a Fremont General Corporation annual report.
フリーモント・ジェネラル社のアニュアルリポートより、本文中の写真などの要素と調和がとれるよう留意して制作された財務関連のグラフ。

KUWAIT REAL ESTATE COMPANY
ENGLAND 1982
CD,AD,D:Alan Fletcher
D:Paul Anthony/Gill Davies
DF:Pentagram Design Ltd.

STATISTICAL
TABLES & GRAPHS

CHARTS & SCORES

MAPS

ARCHITECTURAL
PLANS & DRAWINGS

INSTRUCTIONAL DIAGRAMS
FOR PRODUCTS

SCIENTIFIC
ILLUSTRATIONS

Graphs illustrating the financial position of a real estate company. From a Kuwait Real Estate Company annual report.
クウェート不動産会社のアニュアルリポートより、同社の財政状態を表すグラフ。

STATISTICAL
TABLES & GRAPHS

CHARTS & SCORES

MAPS

ARCHITECTURAL
PLANS & DRAWINGS

INSTRUCTIONAL DIAGRAMS
FOR PRODUCTS

SCIENTIFIC
ILLUSTRATIONS

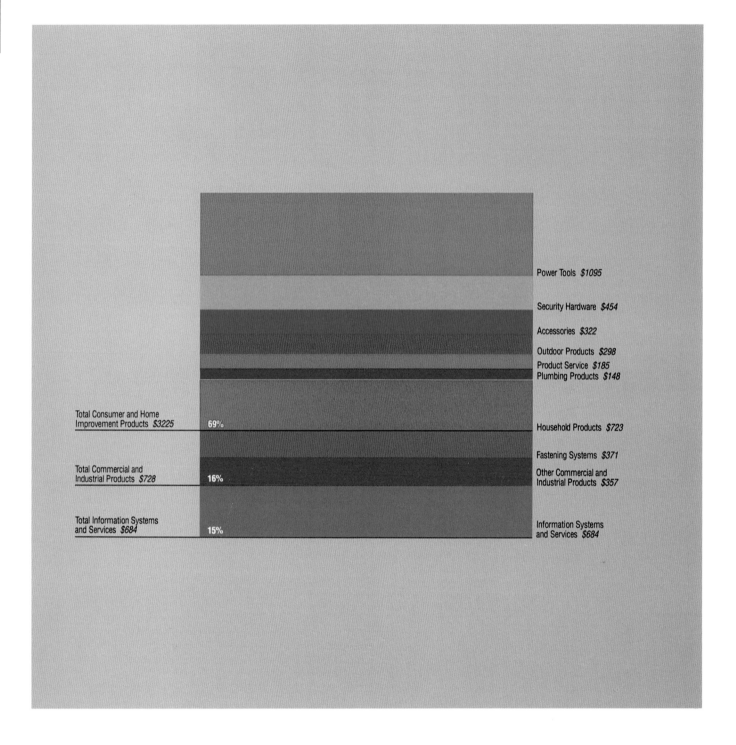

アニュアルリポートより、1991年度ブラック&デッカー社の全世界からの歳入を表したグラフ。

Power Tools *$1095*

Security Hardware *$454*

Accessories *$322*

Outdoor Products *$298*
Product Service *$185*
Plumbing Products *$148*

Total Consumer and Home
Improvement Products *$3225*   69%   Household Products *$723*

Fastening Systems *$371*

Total Commercial and
Industrial Products *$728*   16%   Other Commercial and
Industrial Products *$357*

Total Information Systems
and Services *$684*   15%   Information Systems
and Services *$684*

Black & Decker 1991 worldwide revenues, in millions of dollars. From an annual report.
アニュアルリポートより、1991年度ブラック&デッカー社の全世界からの歳入を表したグラフ。

STATISTICAL
TABLES & GRAPHS

CHARTS & SCORES

MAPS

ARCHITECTURAL
PLANS & DRAWINGS

INSTRUCTIONAL DIAGRAMS
FOR PRODUCTS

SCIENTIFIC
ILLUSTRATIONS

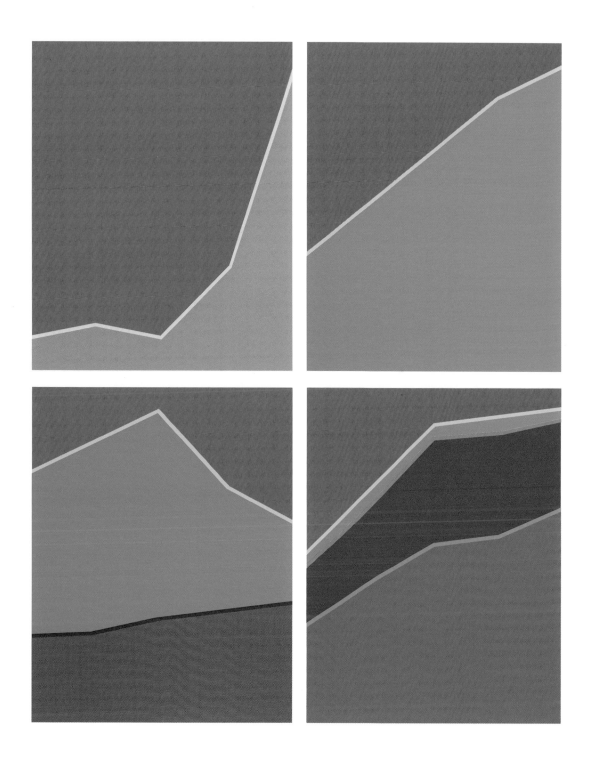

Fiscal graphs as part of the overall design of the color spread. From a Lockheed Corporation annual report.
ロッキード社のアニュアルリポートより、配色に工夫して表現した財務に関するグラフ。

MEDICAL INTER-INSURANCE EXCHANGE
OF NEW JERSEY
USA 1992
AD:Roger Cook/Don Shanosky
D:Cathryn L. Cook
DF:Cook and Shanosky Associates, Inc.

STATISTICAL
TABLES & GRAPHS

CHARTS & SCORES

MAPS

ARCHITECTURAL
PLANS & DRAWINGS

INSTRUCTIONAL DIAGRAMS
FOR PRODUCTS

SCIENTIFIC
ILLUSTRATIONS

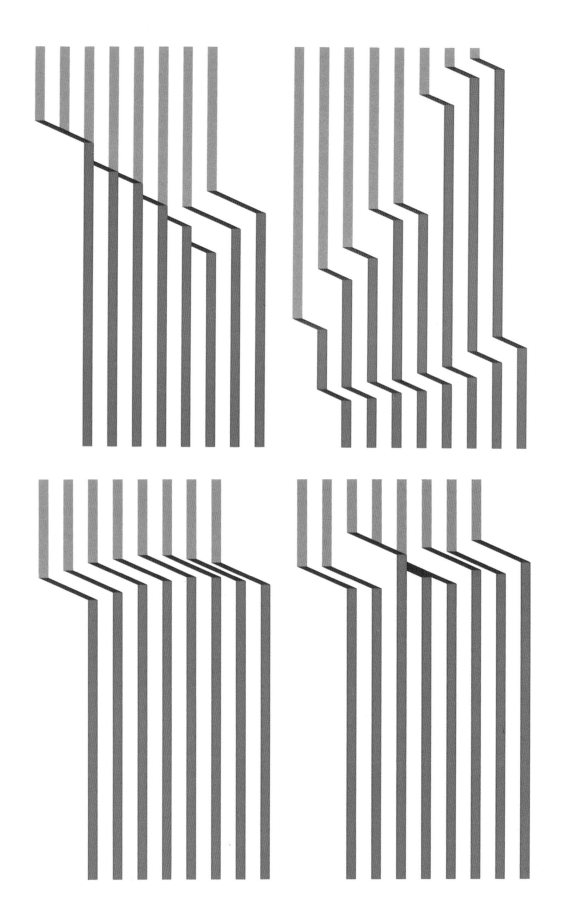

Four medical insurance graphs. From a Medical Inter-Insurance Exchange annual report.
メディカル・インターインシュランス・エスクチェンジ社のアニュアルリポートより、医療保険に関する4つのグラフ。

STATISTICAL
TABLES & GRAPHS

CHARTS & SCORES

MAPS

ARCHITECTURAL
PLANS & DRAWINGS

INSTRUCTIONAL DIAGRAMS
FOR PRODUCTS

SCIENTIFIC
ILLUSTRATIONS

JANNOCK LIMITED
CANADA 1992
AD,D:Roslyn Eskind
D:Sandi King
I:Gary Mansbridge
DF:Eskind Waddell

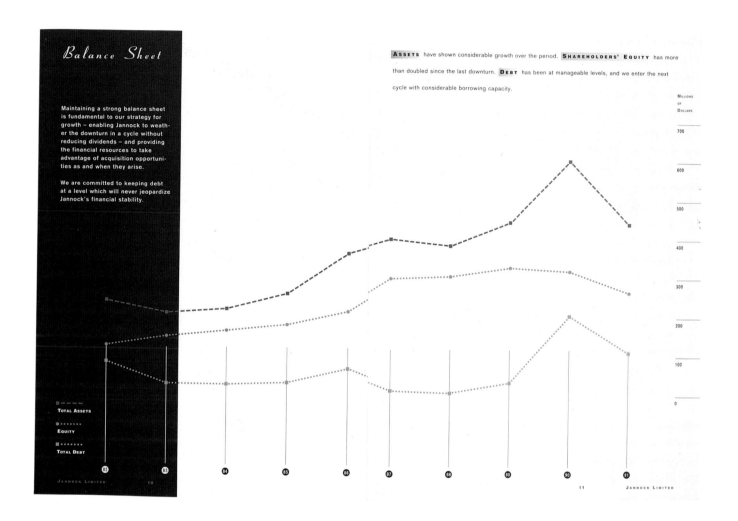

Balance Sheet

Maintaining a strong balance sheet
is fundamental to our strategy for
growth – enabling Jannock to weath-
er the downturn in a cycle without
reducing dividends – and providing
the financial resources to take
advantage of acquisition opportunities as and when they arise.

We are committed to keeping debt
at a level which will never jeopardize
Jannock's financial stability.

TOTAL ASSETS

EQUITY

TOTAL DEBT

JANNOCK LIMITED   10

ASSETS have shown considerable growth over the period. **SHAREHOLDERS' EQUITY** has more
than doubled since the last downturn. **DEBT** has been at manageable levels, and we enter the next
cycle with considerable borrowing capacity.

MILLIONS
OF
DOLLARS

700

600

500

400

300

200

100

0

11   JANNOCK LIMITED

Graph illustrating the company's long-term growth record issued during a down-turn cycle. From a Jannock Limited annual report.
ジャノック社のアニュアルリポートより、不景気時におけるクライアントの長期的な成長を表すグラフ。

STATISTICAL
TABLES & GRAPHS

CHARTS & SCORES

MAPS

ARCHITECTURAL
PLANS & DRAWINGS

INSTRUCTIONAL DIAGRAMS
FOR PRODUCTS

SCIENTIFIC
ILLUSTRATIONS

CENTOCOR, INC.
USA 1987
CD:Charles C. Cabot III
AD,D:Joel Katz
DF:Katz Wheeler Design

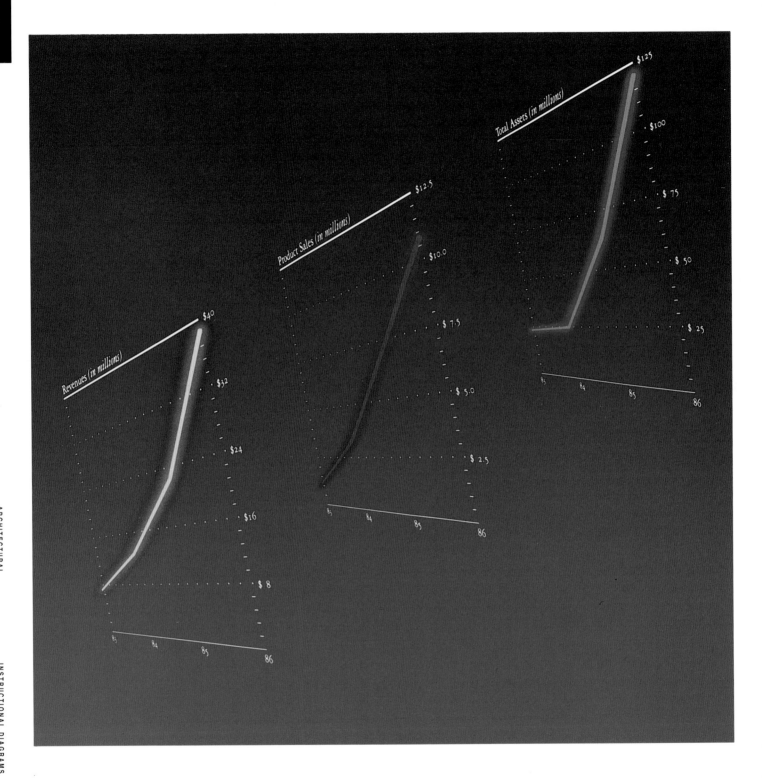

Graph of financial highlights. From a Centocor, Inc. annual report.
セントコア社のアニュアルリポートより、強調して見せたい財務データのグラフ。

STATISTICAL
TABLES &
GRAPHS

CHARTS & SCORES

MAPS

ARCHITECTURAL
PLANS & DRAWINGS

INSTRUCTIONAL DIAGRAMS
FOR PRODUCTS

SCIENTIFIC
ILLUSTRATIONS

1. UNOCAL CORPORATION
USA 1986
CD,AD,I:Ray Engle
D,I:Debra Hampton
DF:Ray Engle & Associates

2. PERMANENT TRUSTEE COMPANY LIMITED
AUSTRALIA 1989
CD,AD:Raymond Bennett
D,I:Joanne Delves
DF:Raymond Bennett Design

3. BAKER HUGHES INCORPORATED
USA 1992
CD:Ron Jefferies
D,I:Scott Lambert
DF:The Jefferies Association

1

アメリカのエネルギー事情の今後"についての雑誌記事より、
原油スポット価格を示したグラフ。

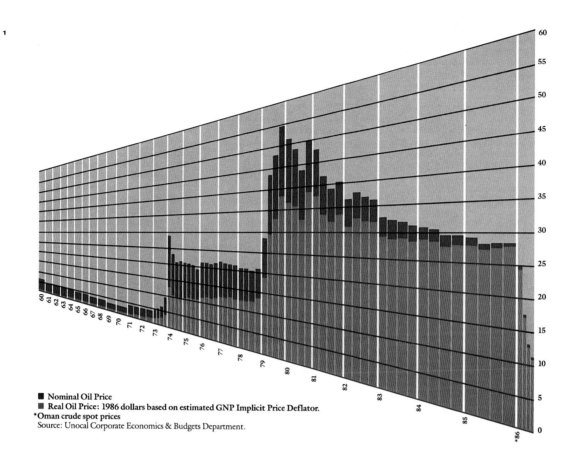

■ Nominal Oil Price
■ Real Oil Price: 1986 dollars based on estimated GNP Implicit Price Deflator.
*Oman crude spot prices
Source: Unocal Corporate Economics & Budgets Department.

2

Shareholders' Funds
$ million

3

1. Graph showing crude oil spot prices.
From a magazine article on America's energy future.
"アメリカのエネルギー事情の今後"についての雑誌記事より、
原油スポット価格を示したグラフ。

2. Graph showing the growth in shareholders' funds
over five years. From a Permanent Trustee
Company Limited annual report.
パーマネント・トラスティー社のアニュアルリポートより、
5カ年内の自己資本の成長ぶりを示すグラフ。

3. Graph of current ratio created to look inspiring during
a down year, hence the broad bases and pointed tops
of the bars. From a Baker Hughes Inc. annual report.
ベーカー・ヒューズ社のアニュアルリポートより、景気下降期を
励ますように楽しい要素を盛り込んだ流動比率のグラフ。

STATISTICAL
TABLES & GRAPHS

CHARTS & SCORES

MAPS

ARCHITECTURAL
PLANS & DRAWINGS

INSTRUCTIONAL DIAGRAMS
FOR PRODUCTS

SCIENTIFIC
ILLUSTRATIONS

Graph showing meteorological data. Appeared on the cover of the architectural magazine, "Building".

建築専門誌「施工」の表紙を飾る、気象データのグラフ。

STATISTICAL
TABLES & GRAPHS

CHARTS & SCORES

MAPS

ARCHITECTURAL
PLANS & DRAWINGS

INSTRUCTIONAL DIAGRAMS
FOR PRODUCTS

SCIENTIFIC
ILLUSTRATIONS

Graph showing "the Regionalization of the Global Economy". From an article in the terminology dictionary, "Basic Knowledge of Contemporary Terminology".
用語辞典「現代用語の基礎知識」の記事より、"世界経済の地域主義化" という題材を効果的に表現するグラフ。

STATISTICAL
TABLES & GRAPHS

CHARTS & SCORES

MAPS

ARCHITECTURAL
PLANS & DRAWINGS

INSTRUCTIONAL DIAGRAMS
FOR PRODUCTS

SCIENTIFIC
ILLUSTRATIONS

SEIYU CO., LTD.
JAPAN 1976
CD,AD,D:Tetsuya Ohta

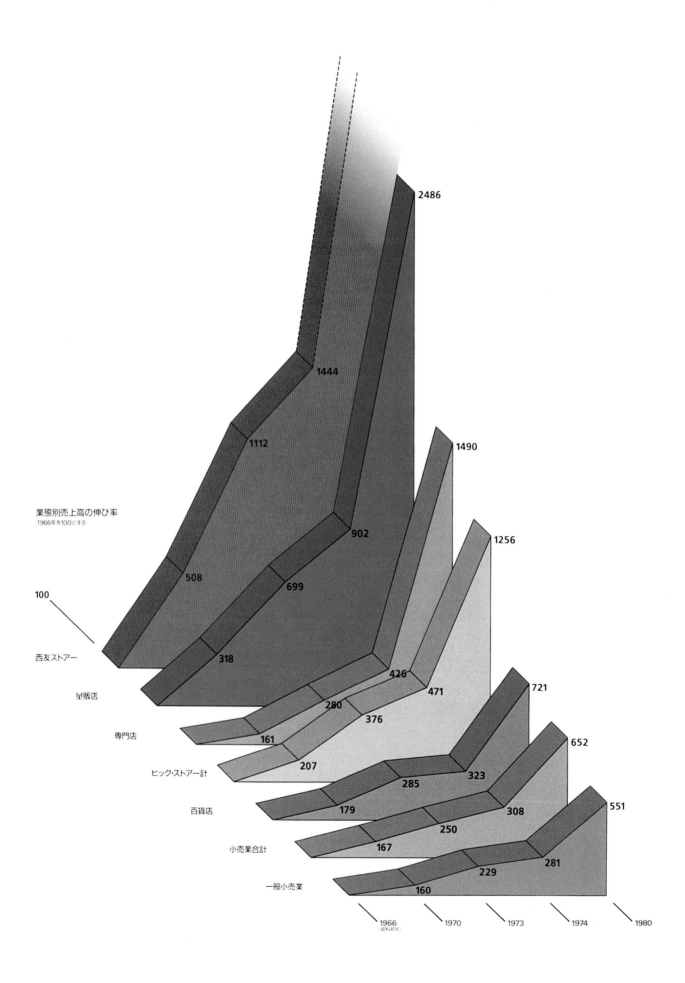

業態別売上高の伸び率
1966年を100とする

100

西友ストアー

量販店

専門店

ビック・ストアー計

百貨店

小売業合計

一般小売業

508   1112   1444   2486

318   699   902   1490

280   426   1256

161   376   471   721

207   285   323   652

179   250   308   551

167   229   281

160

1966
[昭和41年]   1970   1973   1974   1980

Comparison of performance between the supermarket chain Seiyu and other retailers.
スーパーマーケット「西友」の他小売業との業績比較図。

STATISTICAL
TABLES & GRAPHS

CHARTS & SCORES

MAPS

ARCHITECTURAL
PLANS & DRAWINGS

INSTRUCTIONAL DIAGRAMS
FOR PRODUCTS

SCIENTIFIC
ILLUSTRATIONS

SEIYU CO., LTD.
JAPAN 1987
CD,AD,D:Tetsuya Ohta

北海道地区
8店

東北地区
2店

関東地区
144店

中部地区
47店

近畿地区
34店

九州地区
6店

Graph showing the number of stores by region of the supermarket chain, Seiyu.
スーパーマーケット「西友」の地域別店舗数グラフ。

ASSURANCEFORENINGEN
GARD-GJENSIDIG
ENGLAND 1988
CD,AD,D:David Pearce
I:Grundy Northedge
DF:Tatham Pearce

STATISTICAL
TABLES &
GRAPHS

CHARTS & SCORES

MAPS

ARCHITECTURAL
PLANS &
DRAWINGS

INSTRUCTIONAL DIAGRAMS
FOR PRODUCTS

SCIENTIFIC
ILLUSTRATIONS

Table H. Nature of claims (paid claims, gross)

Table F. Balances available to meet outstanding an[d]

to USD 10.4 million (USD 12.2 million). The increase
in funds since 1975 is illustrated in Table F.

As indicated in Note 7 to the Accounts, the funds
available contain a prudent reserve in excess of the
funds needed to meet known and unreported
claims. Unlimited liability, which has been a
cornerstone of the International Group's policy,
places potentially enormous burdens on clubs and
individual shipowners. The Association, therefore,
considers it appropriate that a significant reserve
should be retained against the possibility of the
Association being called upon to meet its share of a
major catastrophe, as well as to meet other
potential liabilities outlined in Note 7.

STATISTICAL
TABLES & GRAPHS

CHARTS & SCORES

MAPS

ARCHITECTURAL
PLANS & DRAWINGS

INSTRUCTIONAL DIAGRAMS
FOR PRODUCTS

SCIENTIFIC
ILLUSTRATIONS

ms. All amounts stated in USD millions.

224.3

190·9

154·5

147·4

125·7

1982 1983 1984 1985 1986

ropriateness of the level of this reserve is
der constant review. Given the lack of any
e in general premium ratings for the last five
nd the recent low or zero rate of contribution,
kely that, unless investment returns remain
t levels, this reserve will continue to

CHANGES IN COVER

were two significant Rule changes at the
of the 1987 policy year and two further
ges in cover, which did not require a change
ıles.

Table E. Estimated cost of notified Pool claims, as
estimated at the following numbers of years after
the start of each policy year (in USD millions).

1 2 3 4 5 6 7

116 119 118 113 127 124
65

1980

42 76 86 92 96 98

1981

41 66 62 58 60

1982

22 48 51 54

1983

26 51 60

1984

36 59

1985

14

1986

Table B. Age of entered vessels
20th February, 1987.

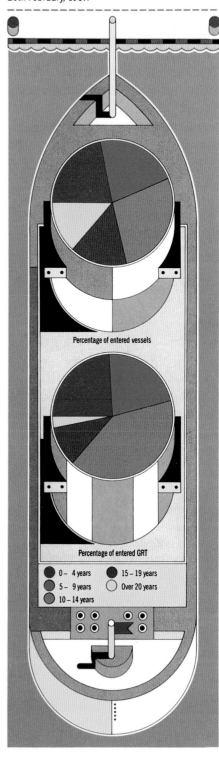

Percentage of entered vessels

Percentage of entered GRT

- 0 – 4 years   - 15 – 19 years
- 5 – 9 years   ○ Over 20 years
- 10 – 14 years

STATISTICAL
TABLES & GRAPHS

CHARTS & SCORES

MAPS

ARCHITECTURAL
PLANS & DRAWINGS

INSTRUCTIONAL DIAGRAMS
FOR PRODUCTS

SCIENTIFIC
ILLUSTRATIONS

$3.482 Tril.

$3.467 Tril.

$3.439 Tril.

M2 (week's end, seasonally adjusted)

Jan.   Feb.   March

USN&WR—Basic data: Federal Reserve Board

January 1991 average
7.04%

6-month CD yields

Dec. 31, 1991
4.26%

Jan. 3, 1992
3201.47

Dow Jones Industrial Average

Dec. 31, 1990
2633.66

National revenue graph and economic index graph. From U.S. News & World Report magazine.
「USニュース＆ワールド・リポートマガジン」より、国家財源および経済指標を表す2つのグラフ。

TREE TOP, INC.
USA 1987
AD,D:John Hornall
D:Luann Bice
I:Bruce Hale
DF:Hornall Anderson Design Works

STATISTICAL TABLES & GRAPHS

CHARTS & SCORES

MAPS

ARCHITECTURAL PLANS & DRAWINGS

INSTRUCTIONAL DIAGRAMS FOR PRODUCTS

SCIENTIFIC ILLUSTRATIONS

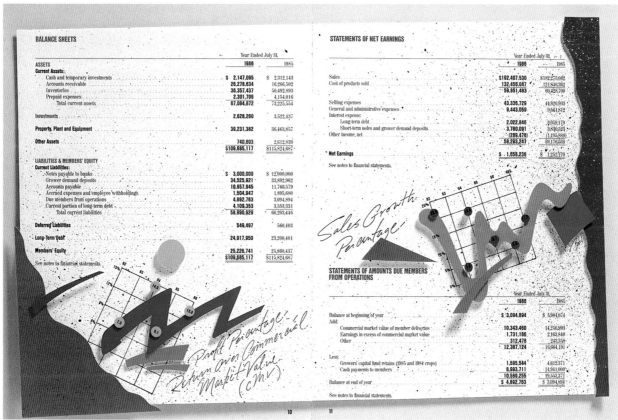

Graphs illustrating performance of an apple growers' co-op. From a Tree Top, Inc. annual report.
ツリートップ社のアニュアルリポートより、リンゴ共同農家組合の業務成績を表したグラフ。

STATISTICAL
TABLES &
GRAPHS

CHARTS & SCORES

MAPS

ARCHITECTURAL
PLANS &
DRAWINGS

INSTRUCTIONAL DIAGRAMS
FOR PRODUCTS

SCIENTIFIC
ILLUSTRATIONS

CAMPAIGN MAGAZINE
ENGLAND 1986,1987
D,I:Peter Grundy/Tilly Northedge
DF:Grundy & Northedge

Statistical diagram from the London ad agency magazine, Campaign.
広告会社向けの専門誌「キャンペーン」に掲載された統計図。

STATISTICAL
TABLES & GRAPHS

CHARTS & SCORES

MAPS

ARCHITECTURAL
PLANS & DRAWINGS

INSTRUCTIONAL DIAGRAMS
FOR PRODUCTS

SCIENTIFIC
ILLUSTRATIONS

DIXON PAPER CENTERS
USA 1988
CD,AD,D:Errol Beauchamp
DF:Beauchamp Group

COMMERCIAL BANK OF KUWAIT
ENGLAND 1979
CD,AD,D:Alan Fletcher
D:Paul Anthony
I:Michael Foreman
DF:Pentagram Design Ltd.

Graph showing financial advantage of purchasing Dixon Paper Centers stocks.
From an advertisement carried in the "Colorado Creative" directory.
名簿録「コロラド・クリエイティブ」に掲載された広告より、
ディクソン・ペーパーセンター社の株を購入した際の利点を伝えるグラフ。

Statistical diagram from a Commercial Bank of Kuwait annual report.
クウェート商業銀行のアニュアルリポートより、統計図表。

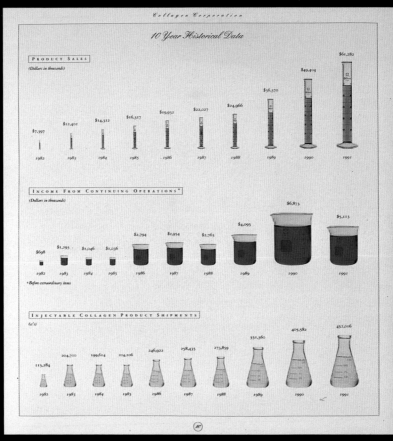

COLLAGEN CORPORATION
USA 1991
CD,AD,D:Earl Gee
D:Fani Chung
P:Geoffrey Nelson
DF:Earl Gee Design

s of the biomedical company's ten-year financial milestones using common scientific measuring devices as picture elements. From a Collagen Corporation annual

生物医学を扱う企業「コラーゲン社」のアニュアルリポートより、研究用の測定用器具をモチーフに同社の過去10年間における財政上重要な出来事を表したグラフ。

AIRBORNE EXPRESS
USA 1992
AD,D:Julia LaPine
D:John Hornall/Heidi Hatlestad
P:Tom Collicott
I,DF:Hornall Anderson Design Works

STATISTICAL
TABLES & GRAPHS

CHARTS & SCORES

MAPS

ARCHITECTURAL
PLANS & DRAWINGS

INSTRUCTIONAL DIAGRAMS
FOR PRODUCTS

SCIENTIFIC
ILLUSTRATIONS

ACTIVE
CUSTOMER
BASE

1991
260,000

1990
233,000

1989
199,000

1988
163,000

1987
126,000

TOTAL SHIPMENTS
(*Thousands*)

1991
108,996

1990
88,220

1989
66,098

1988
47,410

1987
36,157

In these graphs the paper airplanes are symbolic of Airborne Express' worldwide customer base and total shipments. From an Airborne Express annual report.
エアボーン・エクスプレス社を象徴する紙飛行機をモチーフに同社の全世界における顧客数、及び年間輸送量を表したグラフ。

STATISTICAL
TABLES & GRAPHS

CHARTS & SCORES

MAPS

ARCHITECTURAL
PLANS & DRAWINGS

INSTRUCTIONAL DIAGRAMS
FOR PRODUCTS

SCIENTIFIC
ILLUSTRATIONS

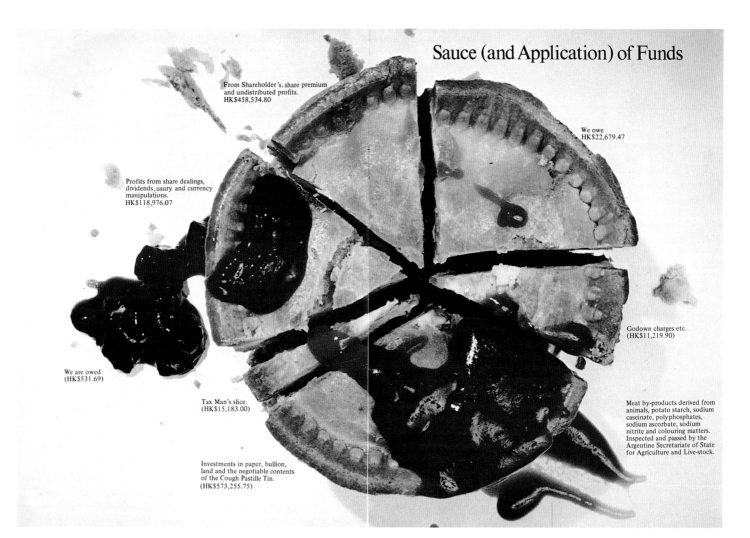

Sauce (and Application) of Funds

From Shareholder's, share premium
and undistributed profits.
HK$458,534.80

We owe
HK$22,679.47

Profits from share dealings,
dividends, usury and currency
manipulations.
HK$118,976.07

Godown charges etc.
(HK$11,219.90)

We are owed
(HK$531.69)

Tax Man's slice.
(HK$15,183.00)

Meat by-products derived from
animals, potato starch, sodium
caseinate, polyphosphates,
sodium ascorbate, sodium
nitrite and colouring matters.
Inspected and passed by the
Argentine Secretariate of State
for Agriculture and Live-stock.

Investments in paper, bullion,
land and the negotiable contents
of the Cough Pastille Tin.
(HK$573,255.75)

Pie graph of source and application of funds. From a TGIF Investments Ltd. annual report.
TGIFインベストメンツ社のアニュアルリポートより、資産の源泉、及び使途や運用の割合を表す円グラフ。

STATISTICAL
TABLES & GRAPHS

CHARTS & SCORES

MAPS

ARCHITECTURAL
PLANS & DRAWINGS

INSTRUCTIONAL DIAGRAMS
FOR PRODUCTS

SCIENTIFIC
ILLUSTRATIONS

SIZZLER RESTAURANTS
INTERNATIONAL INC.
USA 1988
CD,AD:Don Kano
D:Adam Shanosky
P:Art Montes de Oca
DF:Kano Design Group

Restaurants
- Total
- Franchised
- Company operated

587
547
487
464 405
450
372
334
326
311
175 182
153
139 138

84 85 86 87 88

Sales
(monthly sales average, per restaurant, in dollars)
- Company operated
- Franchised

121.8
110.9
105.3
99.8
96.5
89.4
87.8
80.2 80.3
71.5

85 86 87 88

buying and retiring approximately 700,000 shares at an average price of $15.10. Employing the same rationale, in March 1988 our Board authorized a third repurchase of up to 1.7 million shares.

Looking forward, our continuing growth will largely reflect our thorough understanding of the casual dining category — the fastest growing dining segment. We have positioned Sizzler to match America's mood for lighter, fresher tastes as we continue to address the evolving needs of our consumer. The depth of this understanding is perhaps best illustrated by our solid uptrend in customer counts, which rose 6% per store over prior year. In contrast, average industry customer counts, at best, remain flat.

In today's marketplace, the restaurant offering the highest quality products, facilities and services, while presenting the right imagery and best perception of value, will emerge the industry winner. We think Sizzler is that concept.

During fiscal 1988 Sizzler Executive Vice President Michael M. Minchin, Jr. was elected to the Company's Board. His contributions in the areas of marketing, product development and advertising have been significant.

The contributions of our employees and franchisees for the year were no less stellar, as success in the face of a somewhat sluggish industry is not easy to achieve. Extraordinary success under the same conditions is even harder!

Finally, we thank our stockholders, whose support we consider invaluable.

We are anxious to sustain — and improve on — Sizzler's performance in the years ahead. Employing our time-honed success formula, we feel confident of achieving nothing less.

James A. Collins
Chairman of the Board

Richard P. Bermingham
Vice Chairman of the Board

Thomas L. Gregory
President and Chief Executive Officer

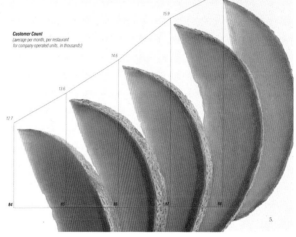

Customer Count
(average per month, per restaurant
for company operated units, in thousands)

16.1
15.9
14.6
13.6
12.7

84 85 86 87 88

5.

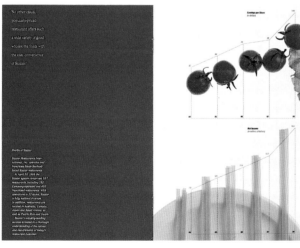

'No other casual, popularly-priced restaurant offers such a wide variety of good wholesome foods with the easy convenience of Sizzler.'

Profile of Sizzler

Sizzler Restaurants International, Inc. operates and franchises Steak-Seafood Salad Sizzler restaurants.

Earnings per Share
(in dollars)

Net Income
(in millions of dollars)

TO OUR STOCKHOLDERS

Revenues
(in millions of dollars)

Pre-Tax Income
(in millions of dollars)

Systemwide Sales
(in millions of dollars)

Graphs using food as a picture element. From the Sizzler Restaurants International Inc. annual report.
シズラーレストランのアニュアルリポートより、食品をモチーフにデザインされたグラフ。

DEUTSCHE
GENOSSENSCHAFTS-HYPOTHEKENBANK
GERMANY 1989
AD,I:Achim Kiel
P:Uwe Brandes
DF:Pencil Corporate Art

STATISTICAL
TABLES & GRAPHS

CHARTS & SCORES

MAPS

ARCHITECTURAL
PLANS & DRAWINGS

INSTRUCTIONAL DIAGRAMS
FOR PRODUCTS

SCIENTIFIC
ILLUSTRATIONS

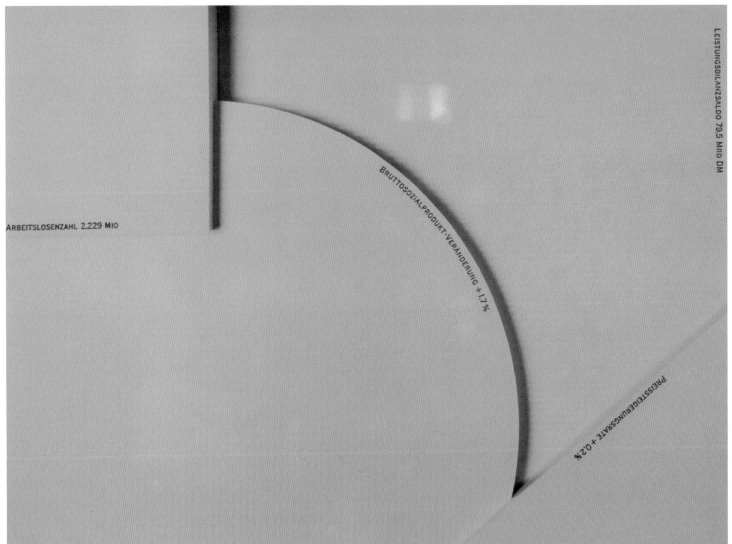

Series of banking diagrams showing financial data. From a Deutsche Genossenschafts-Hypothekenbank business report.
ドイツ組合銀行のビジネスリポートより、財務データを表すグラフシリーズ。

SULLIVAN DENTAL PRODUCTS INC.
USA 1992
CD,AD,D:Gary Haas
P:John Niehuis
DF:Professional Marketing Services

STATISTICAL
TABLES & GRAPHS

CHARTS & SCORES

MAPS

ARCHITECTURAL
PLANS & DRAWINGS

INSTRUCTIONAL DIAGRAMS
FOR PRODUCTS

SCIENTIFIC
ILLUSTRATIONS

Graphs showing growth in equipment sales & service centers, customer accounts and sales force of a distributor of dental supplies and equipment.

From a Sullivan Dental Products, Inc. annual report.

サリバン・デンタルプロダクツ社のアニュアルリポートより、歯科治療機器や補給品を取り扱う販売会社の売上高・サービスセンター数、得意先数、販売力などを表すグラフ。

STATISTICAL TABLES & GRAPHS

CHARTS & SCORES

MAPS

ARCHITECTURAL PLANS & DRAWINGS

INSTRUCTIONAL DIAGRAMS FOR PRODUCTS

SCIENTIFIC ILLUSTRATIONS

1. BBC
ENGLAND 1991
CD:Helen Alexiou
AD,D:Philip Kruger
P:Dave Denham

2. REED BUSINESS CALL
ENGLAND 1989
CD:Helen Alexiou
D:Philip Kruger
P:Jerome Zimmerman

3. INTERNATIONAL DISTILLERS & VINTNERS
ENGLAND 1991
CD,AD,D,I:Philip Kruger
P:Dave Denham

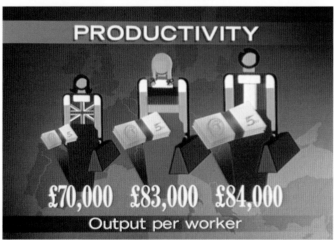

**4. 6. BBC TELEVISION, NEWS
AND CURRENT AFFAIRS**
ENGLAND 1992
D:Robert Shergold/Jean Cramond
DF:N/CA Graphic Design Department

5. THE PRESENTATION COMPANY
ENGLAND 1991
CD,AD,D,I:Philip Kruger
P:Dave Denham

STATISTICAL
TABLES & GRAPHS

CHARTS & SCORES

MAPS

ARCHITECTURAL
PLANS & DRAWINGS

INSTRUCTIONAL DIAGRAMS
FOR PRODUCTS

SCIENTIFIC
ILLUSTRATIONS

1. CHANNEL 4 TELEVISION
ENGLAND 1991
CD,AD,D,I:Richard Schedler
P:Dave Denham

**2. 3. 4. 5. BBC TELEVISION, NEWS
AND CURRENT AFFAIRS**
ENGLAND 1992
D:Steve Aspinall/Kate Finding/
Bill Calder/Kaye Huddy
DF:News & Current Affairs
Graphic Design Dept.

6. INHOUSE
ENGLAND 1992
CD,AD,D,I:Philip Kruger
P:Dave Denham

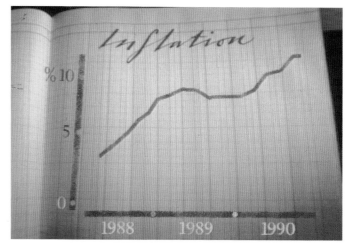

Visualized graphs produced for corporate or TV presentation.
テレビ番組や企業のプレゼンテーションの映像用に制作されたグラフ。

BRITISH GAS PLC
ENGLAND 1990
CD:Geoff Aldridge
AD,D,I:Duncan Wilson
I:Barry Brocklebank
DF:Communication by Design

STATISTICAL TABLES & GRAPHS

CHARTS & SCORES

MAPS

ARCHITECTURAL PLANS & DRAWINGS

INSTRUCTIONAL DIAGRAMS FOR PRODUCTS

SCIENTIFIC ILLUSTRATIONS

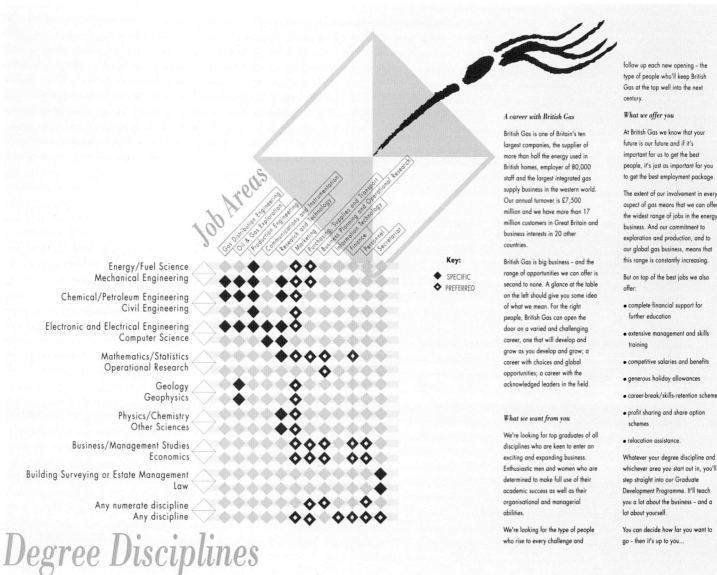

Key:
◆ SPECIFIC
◇ PREFERRED

A career with British Gas

British Gas is one of Britain's ten largest companies, the supplier of more than half the energy used in British homes, employer of 80,000 staff and the largest integrated gas supply business in the western world. Our annual turnover is £7,500 million and we have more than 17 million customers in Great Britain and business interests in 20 other countries.

British Gas is big business – and the range of opportunities we can offer is second to none. A glance at the table on the left should give you some idea of what we mean. For the right people, British Gas can open the door on a varied and challenging career, one that will develop and grow as you develop and grow; a career with choices and global opportunities; a career with the acknowledged leaders in the field.

What we want from you

We're looking for top graduates of all disciplines who are keen to enter an exciting and expanding business. Enthusiastic men and women who are determined to make full use of their academic success as well as their organisational and managerial abilities.

We're looking for the type of people who rise to every challenge and follow up each new opening – the type of people who'll keep British Gas at the top well into the next century.

What we offer you

At British Gas we know that your future is our future and if it's important for us to get the best people, it's just as important for you to get the best employment package.

The extent of our involvement in every aspect of gas means that we can offer the widest range of jobs in the energy business. And our commitment to exploration and production, and to our global gas business, means that this range is constantly increasing.

But on top of the best jobs we also offer:

- complete financial support for further education

- extensive management and skills training

- competitive salaries and benefits

- generous holiday allowances

- career-break/skills-retention scheme

- profit sharing and share option schemes

- relocation assistance.

Whatever your degree discipline and whichever area you start out in, you'll step straight into our Graduate Development Programme. It'll teach you a lot about the business – and a lot about yourself.

You can decide how far you want to go – then it's up to you…

Degree/discipline matrix table showing graduates the job areas appropriate to their particular qualifications. From a British Gas PLC. recruitment guide.
ブリティッシュ・ガス社の就職案内より、卒業生の取得資格に見合った職業分野を知らせるための学位・専門科目行列表。

STATISTICAL
TABLES & GRAPHS

CHARTS & SCORES

MAPS

ARCHITECTURAL
PLANS & DRAWINGS

INSTRUCTIONAL DIAGRAMS
FOR PRODUCTS

SCIENTIFIC
ILLUSTRATIONS

[RIG RENTSCH]
TRIMBACH, SWITZERLAND
SWITZERLAND 1988
CD,AD,D,I:Michael Baviera
DF:BBV Michael Baviera

[RIG RENTSCH]

Anteile am konsolidierten Umsatz.

Anteil am konsolidierten Umsatz nach Ländern						
in Fr. 1000	in %					
8 504	3,5	übrige				
24 786	10,2		Frankreich			
26 730	11,0			Benelux		
46 412	19,1				Schweiz	
49 328	20,3					England
87 236	35,9					BRD

13

Graph showing break down of consolidated turnover. From a Rig Rentsch annual report.
リグレンチ社のアニュアルリポートより、複合出来高の内訳を表したグラフ。

STATISTICAL
TABLES & GRAPHS

CHARTS & SCORES

MAPS

ARCHITECTURAL
PLANS & DRAWINGS

INSTRUCTIONAL DIAGRAMS
FOR PRODUCTS

SCIENTIFIC
ILLUSTRATIONS

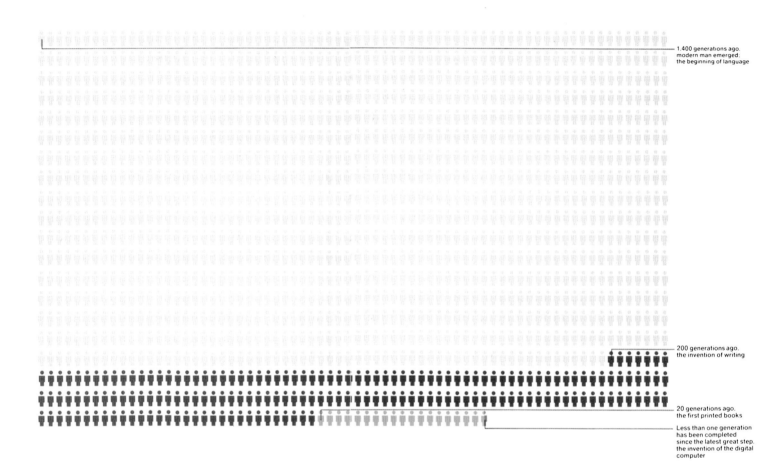

1,400 generations ago.
modern man emerged:
the beginning of language

200 generations ago.
the invention of writing

20 generations ago.
the first printed books

Less than one generation
has been completed
since the latest great step.
the invention of the digital
computer

Chart illustrating the history of the development of human communication.
人類の情報伝達手段の発展を歴史的に表すチャート。

STATISTICAL
TABLES & GRAPHS

CHARTS & SCORES

MAPS

ARCHITECTURAL
PLANS & DRAWINGS

INSTRUCTIONAL DIAGRAMS
FOR PRODUCTS

SCIENTIFIC
ILLUSTRATIONS

JIYU KOKUMIN-SHA
JAPAN 1988
AD:Tokihiro Okuda
D:Mitsuko Kato/Kumiko Yamagami
I:Fumiyo Kojima

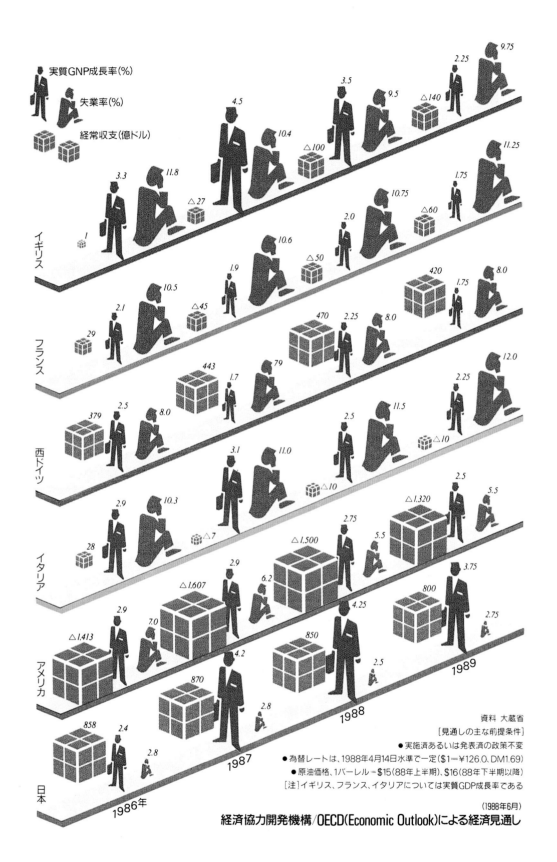

経済協力開発機構/OECD(Economic Outlook)による経済見通し

資料 大蔵省
[見通しの主な前提条件]
● 実施済あるいは発表済の政策不変
● 為替レートは、1988年4月14日水準で一定($1=¥126.0、DM1.69)
● 原油価格、1バーレル=$15(88年上半期)、$16(88年下半期以降)
[注]イギリス、フランス、イタリアについては実質GDP成長率である

(1988年6月)

Graph showing economic conditions in various countries based on data provided by the OECD.
From an article in the terminology dictionary, "Basic Knowledge of Contemporary Terminology".
用語辞典「現代用語の基礎知識」の記事より、経済協力機構(OECD)による世界各国の経済状況見通しを表すグラフ。

STATISTICAL
TABLES & GRAPHS

CHARTS & SCORES

MAPS

ARCHITECTURAL
PLANS & DRAWINGS

INSTRUCTIONAL DIAGRAMS
FOR PRODUCTS

SCIENTIFIC
ILLUSTRATIONS

CENTOCOR, INC.
USA 1991
CD:Stephen Ferrari
D:John Ball
I:Michael Crumpton/
Martin Haggland/Micro Color
DF:The Graphic Expression, Inc.

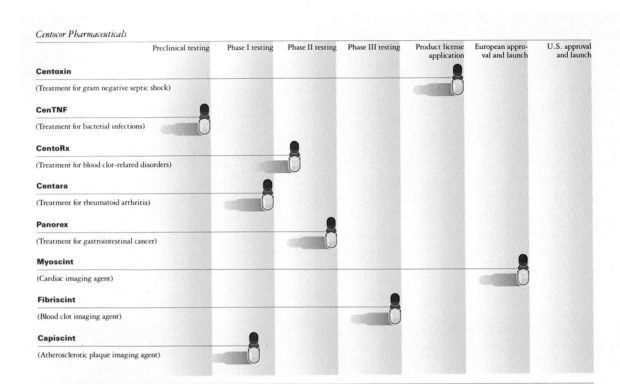

Centocor Pharmaceuticals

	Preclinical testing	Phase I testing	Phase II testing	Phase III testing	Product license application	European approval and launch	U.S. approval and launch

Centoxin
(Treatment for gram negative septic shock)

CenTNF
(Treatment for bacterial infections)

CentoRx
(Treatment for blood clot-related disorders)

Centara
(Treatment for rheumatoid arthritis)

Panorex
(Treatment for gastrointestinal cancer)

Myoscint
(Cardiac imaging agent)

Fibriscint
(Blood clot imaging agent)

Capiscint
(Atherosclerotic plaque imaging agent)

Centocor Diagnostics

	Development	Release for research use	First commercial sale

CA 125
(Ovarian cancer test)

CA 19-9
(Pancreatic cancer test)

CA 15-3
(Breast cancer test)

CA 72-4
(Gastric cancer test)

P-glycoCHEK
(Multidrug resistance test)

This chart is a representation of the company's drug "Pipeline" showing the product line and where in the process each product is currently. From a Centocor Inc. annual report.
セントコア社のアニュアルリポートより、同社の医薬製品「パイプライン」の製造過程を表した図。

BNN CO.
JAPAN 1992
AD,D:Sonoe Takigami

STATISTICAL
TABLES & GRAPHS

CHARTS & SCORES

MAPS

ARCHITECTURAL
PLANS & DRAWINGS

INSTRUCTIONAL DIAGRAMS
FOR PRODUCTS

SCIENTIFIC
ILLUSTRATIONS

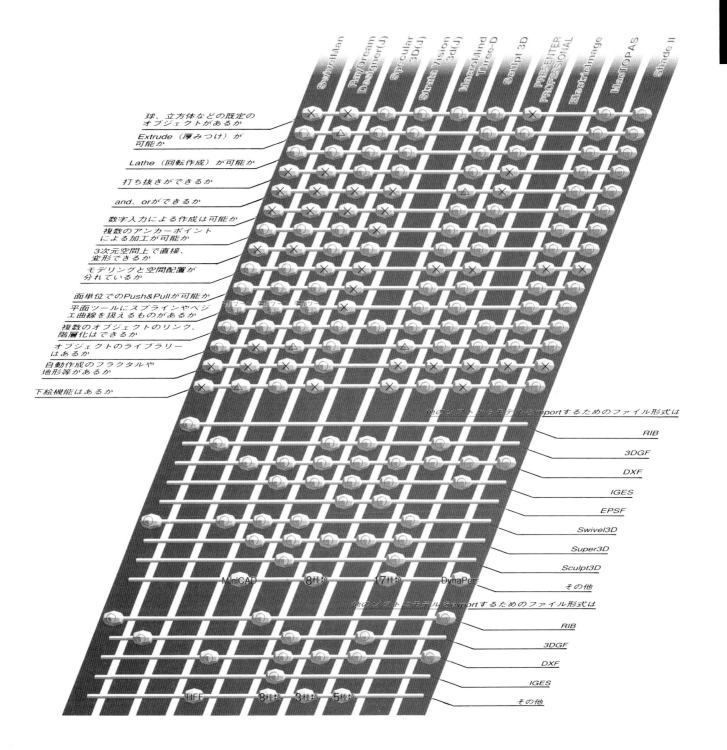

Comparison table of 3-D modelling functions in graphics software programs for the Macintosh computer. From Maclife magazine.
月刊誌「マックライフ」より、マッキントッシュ・コンピューターの3Dグラフィックソフト・モデリング機能比較表。

STATISTICAL TABLES & GRAPHS

CHARTS & SCORES

MAPS

ARCHITECTURAL PLANS & DRAWINGS

INSTRUCTIONAL DIAGRAMS FOR PRODUCTS

SCIENTIFIC ILLUSTRATIONS

IBM JAPAN, LTD.
JAPAN 1990, 1991
CD:Haruo Yoshida
AD:Jun Tabohashi
D:Seijo Kawaguchi/
Nobukuni Takada
P:Yutaka Sakano
PR:Hideo Wakana

Graphs based upon a photo for forecasting the emissions of CO2 and the average age in various countries in the year 2000.
日本IBM社の企業広告より、2000年における各国の二酸化炭素の排出量、及び平均年齢の予測を写真で表現したグラフ。

BLUEPRINT MAGAZINE

ENGLAND 1992

D,I:Peter Grundy/

Tilly Northedge

DF:Grundy & Northedge

Information Designers

STATISTICAL
TABLES & GRAPHS

CHARTS & SCORES

MAPS

ARCHITECTURAL
PLANS & DRAWINGS

INSTRUCTIONAL DIAGRAMS
FOR PRODUCTS

SCIENTIFIC
ILLUSTRATIONS

DOUGHNUT LONDON
Three decades that saw a city explode

A rapid shift in population has made old definitions of London redundant. The defunct Greater London Council was a belated attempt in the 1960s to catch up with the fact that the city had spilled far beyond the boundaries of what is now called inner London. But even then, the focus of the capital was already shifting further and further towards its edges, into the nebulously defined metropolitan area and beyond.

Visual magazine "Blueprint" article detailing social changes in London over the last 30 years.

ビジュアル雑誌「ブルー・プリント」の記事より、過去30年におけるロンドンの社会変化を詳細に表しているダイアグラム。

ELECTRICAL & ELECTRONIC
INSULATION ASSOCIATION - (EEIA)
ENGLAND 1992
D:Ian Moore

INTERNATIONAL PLANNED
PARENTHOOD FEDERATION
ENGLAND 1990
CD,AD,D,I:Tilly Northedge
DF:Grundy & Northedge

STATISTICAL
TABLES & GRAPHS

CHARTS & SCORES

MAPS

ARCHITECTURAL
PLANS & DRAWINGS

INSTRUCTIONAL DIAGRAMS
FOR PRODUCTS

SCIENTIFIC
ILLUSTRATIONS

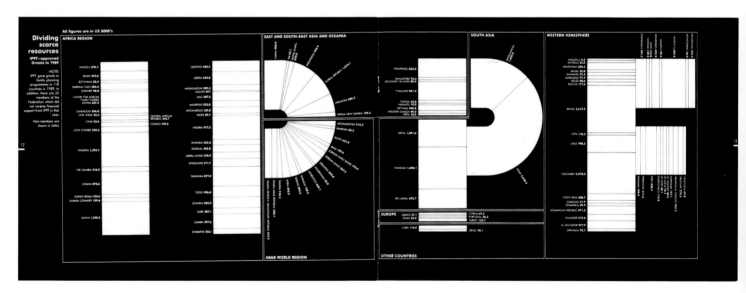

A comprehensive guide to the members of the
"Electrical & Electronic Insulation Association" (EEIA, London) and their range of products.
ロンドンのエレクトリカル＆エレクトロニック・インシュレイション協会（EEIA）のメンバー、
及び製品群についての総合案内図。

Financial graph for International Planned Parenthood Federation (IPPF)
from an annual report.
国際家族計画連盟（IPPF）のアニュアルリポートより、財務に関するグラフ。

**SATELLITE DIGITAL AUDIO
BROADCASTING CO., LTD.**
JAPAN 1991
CD:Ryozo Tada/Sho Akiyama
AD:Gan Hosoya
D:Haruto Takanashi
P:Kazuyoshi Miyoshi

STATISTICAL
TABLES & GRAPHS

CHARTS & SCORES

MAPS

ARCHITECTURAL
PLANS & DRAWINGS

INSTRUCTIONAL DIAGRAMS
FOR PRODUCTS

SCIENTIFIC
ILLUSTRATIONS

Program table (tide table at the satellite TV station St. Giga) which schedules its programming according to the tides.

潮の満ち引き（タイド）にあわせて時間帯を設定し番組を放送する衛星TV局St. GIGAの番組表（タイドテーブル）。

STATISTICAL
TABLES & GRAPHS

CHARTS & SCORES

MAPS

ARCHITECTURAL
PLANS & DRAWINGS

INSTRUCTIONAL DIAGRAMS
FOR PRODUCTS

SCIENTIFIC
ILLUSTRATIONS

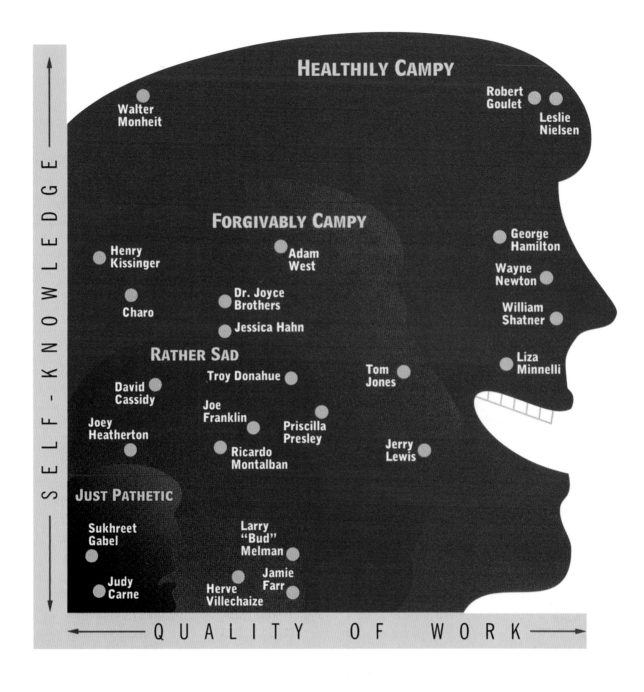

Celebrity-delusion index. Who's "in" and knows it, and who's "out" but does not know it! From Spy magazine.
「スパイマガジン」より、有名人の勘違い指数を表したグラフ。

チャート & スコア

データ相互の関係や流れを、グラフに較べて、より自由な形式で視覚化したダイアグラムが、チャートとスコアである。

チャートの基本は、図による式、すなわち図式にある。時間的に一方向にしか流れない文章表現に対して、空間的に多方向に展開する視覚表現がチャートである、ともいえる。

その応用範囲は、概念や論理の構造を示す図式からはじまって、それをモデル化する模式図、相互関係を示す関係図、変化の様相を示す過程図から、組織的な構造を示す組織図、系図や進化系統樹のような系統図に至るまで、きわめて広範囲に及んでいる。ともかく、文字づらだけを追っていたのでは内容を把握しにくいデータの相互関係や構造を、視覚的なイメージとして解説するのがチャートの目的である。

チャートには、表やグラフのような、データの配置上の明確なルールがないケースも多い。したがって、デザイナーの仕事も、ダイアグラムの視覚的な面白さとデータの読み取りやすさを両立させるための、デザイン上のルール作りから始まることになる。

画面が複雑になりがちなのが、このダイアグラムの特徴でもあるので、ある程度以上の数の記号を使用する際などには、地図の凡例にあたる、「読み方のルール一覧」をどこかで明示する親切さも忘れないようにしたい。

スコアは、楽譜や年譜のように、時間などの流れと、その流れに沿ったデータの変化を視覚的に記述したもののことである。

変化を表わすということでは、既に紹介したグラフなども有力な手段ではあったが、同じ「変化」の図解であっても、グラフがその「量」の変化を表示しているのに対して、スコアは、楽譜の例からもわかる通り、その「質」の変化の方を表示するものである。

したがって、スコアでは、グラフのように、視覚的に数量化された線や面のデザイン要素と、「質」を記述するための文字や記号の複合的な表現が見られ、内容的にも広がりの大きな画面が形成されることも多い。

チャートやグラフのようには多くの作例は見られないダイアグラムながら、スコアというものには視覚表現としてのダイアグラムの大きな可能性が秘められているといえよう。

CHARTS & SCORES

CHARTS & SCORES.

A diagram that needs to visualize the interrelations of data and the flow of changing data requires a somewhat more free-form approach. These diagrams are called charts or scores. Basically, a chart is a formula that has been schematized graphically. In other words, a chart is a visual expression that evolves in many directions at once. The chart uses space for this purpose, as opposed to written notation because writing flows in only one direction in time and space, and so has difficulty in expressing the dynamics required.

The range of application for charts and scores is, not surprisingly, very wide. It may be a simple schematic to indicate a basic concept and its logical structure. Where a generalization is drawn from a model, it may be charted so that the relationships are indicated. Flow-charts in which the sequence and vectors of change are tracked graphically. Organizational charts that indicate the structure of organizations through systematic spatial arrangements, such as family trees, evolutionary charts etc. The purpose of the chart is to describe correspondences in the structure of data which would otherwise be quite difficult to grasp. The complex interplay of forces that can be easily demonstrated in a chart may be virtually impossible to convey with a narrative of written text or numerical expression. The designer's task starts with establishing a set of graphic design rules so that both visual appeal and readability can be achieved. The problem inherent to this type of diagram is that it can easily become too complicated and crowded. If the designer is going to use more than a certain minimum number of symbols, then he must remember to provide the viewer with "list of symbols" such as the legends seen in maps.

チャート & スコア

A score is a visual description of the flow of changes in data, often along a time line. This includes musical scores, chronological records and so forth. Speaking of describing changes, a graph is also an effective means to do this, but there is a difference. Both graphs and scores illustrate "change" but while the graph indicates a quantitative change, the score as you can clearly see in the example of a musical score, indicates changes in quality. In a score, therefore, one sees a combination of expressive devices and design elements such as lines and surfaces which provide visual quality as well as characters and symbols which are used to describe the "quantities". Thus, a score can represent a vast range of content. A score is a type of diagram which, although not seen so often, still represents enormous possibilities for the visual expression of complex data.

STATISTICAL
TABLES & GRAPHS

CHARTS & SCORES

MAPS

ARCHITECTURAL
PLANS & DRAWINGS

INSTRUCTIONAL DIAGRAMS
FOR PRODUCTS

SCIENTIFIC
ILLUSTRATIONS

HORNALL ANDERSON DESIGN WORKS
USA 1990
AD,D:Jack Anderson
DF:Hornall Anderson Design Works

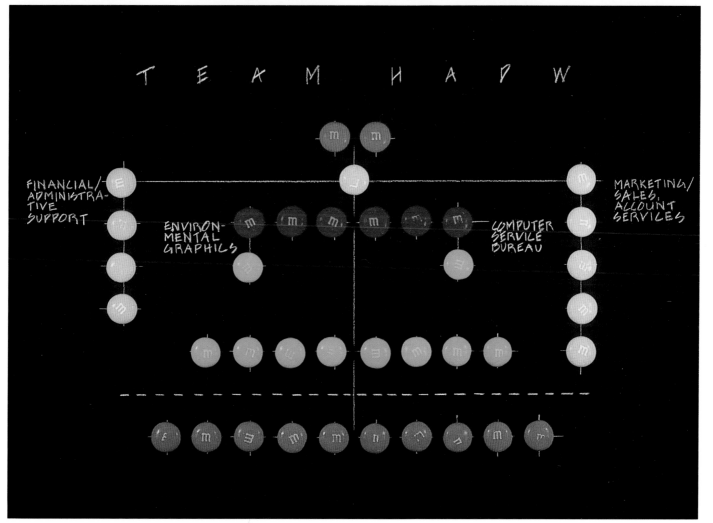

Company organization charts by Hornall Anderson Design Works.
ホーネルアンダーソン・デザインワークスによる会社組織図。

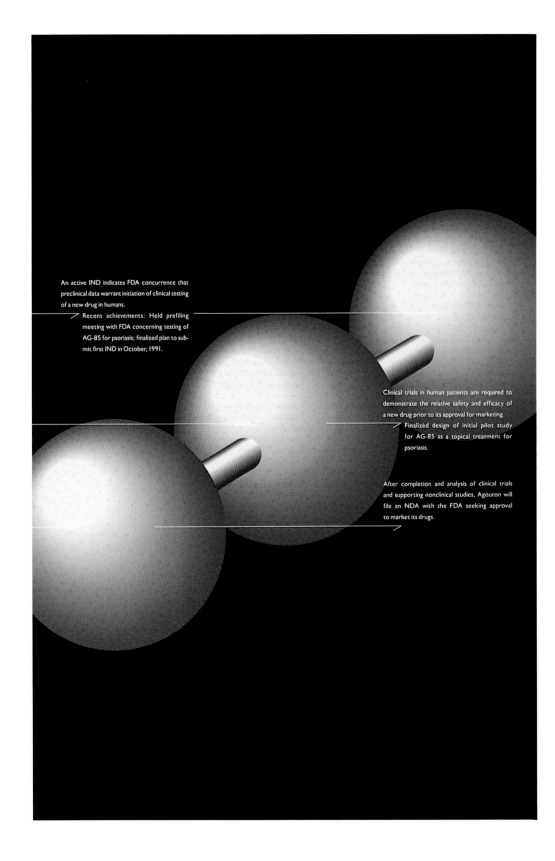

STATISTICAL
TABLES & GRAPHS

CHARTS & SCORES

MAPS

ARCHITECTURAL
PLANS & DRAWINGS

INSTRUCTIONAL DIAGRAMS
FOR PRODUCTS

SCIENTIFIC
ILLUSTRATIONS

AGOURON PHARMACEUTICALS, INC.
USA 1991
AD,D,I:Rik Besser
AD:Douglas Joseph
I:Koji Takei
DF:Besser Joseph Partners, Inc.

An active IND indicates FDA concurrence that preclinical data warrant initiation of clinical testing of a new drug in humans.

Recent achievements: Held prefiling meeting with FDA concerning testing of AG-85 for psoriasis; finalized plan to submit first IND in October, 1991.

Clinical trials in human patients are required to demonstrate the relative safety and efficacy of a new drug prior to its approval for marketing.

Finalized design of initial pilot study for AG-85 as a topical treatment for psoriasis.

After completion and analysis of clinical trials and supporting nonclinical studies, Agouron will file an NDA with the FDA seeking approval to market its drugs.

1. Investigational New Drug Application (IND)

2. Clinical Trials

3. New Drug Application (NDA)

STATISTICAL TABLES & GRAPHS

CHARTS & SCORES

MAPS

ARCHITECTURAL PLANS & DRAWINGS

INSTRUCTIONAL DIAGRAMS FOR PRODUCTS

SCIENTIFIC ILLUSTRATIONS

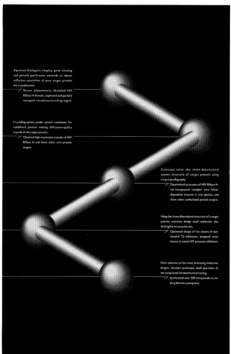

Chart based on molecular models designed to represent the company's drug development process. From an Agouron Pharmaceuticals Inc. annual report.

アグーロン製薬会社のアニュアルリポートより、薬品開発のプロセスを分子モデルをモチーフにして表したチャート。

STATISTICAL
TABLES & GRAPHS

CHARTS & SCORES

MAPS

ARCHITECTURAL
PLANS & DRAWINGS

INSTRUCTIONAL DIAGRAMS
FOR PRODUCTS

SCIENTIFIC
ILLUSTRATIONS

Chart delineating SpaceLabs patient care management system capabilities past (the overlay) and present.
Chart and accompanying overlay capture a variety of significant points in the development of high definition imaging created by Advanced Technology Laboratories.
From a Westmark International annual report.
ウエストマーク・インターナショナル社のアニュアルリポートより、「スペースラブ」の過去から現在までの看護管理システムの能力を表したチャート、
及びアドバンスドテクノロジー・ラボラトリーズ社が制作した高品位映像の開発説明図。

NATIONAL MEDICAL ENTERPRISES, INC.
USA 1991
CD:Ron Jefferies
D,I:Claudia Jefferies
DF:The Jefferies Association

STATISTICAL
TABLES & GRAPHS

CHARTS & SCORES

MAPS

ARCHITECTURAL
PLANS & DRAWINGS

INSTRUCTIONAL DIAGRAMS
FOR PRODUCTS

SCIENTIFIC
ILLUSTRATIONS

Discharge Planning Phase
As the end of the hospital
stay approaches, a plan for
continuing outpatient care
may be formulated, and a
final regimen of medication
is determined. Then, the
patient leaves the hospital,
prepared to return to a productive life with new skills
and renewed self-confidence.

Skills Development Phase
There are two goals in the
skills development phase,
one is to educate the patient
to the biochemical nature
of depression and establish
therapeutic levels of medication. The other is to develop
new behavior skills. A variety of individual and group
therapies is employed, up to
six hours a day, seven days a
week.

Treatment Planning
The multidisciplinary treatment team is assembled.
With the patient's participation, specific goals are
established for addressing
behavioral problems and
correcting biochemical
imbalances.

Diagnostic Phase
After a patient is admitted
to the hospital by a psychi-
atrist, a comprehensive
battery of biological and
psychological tests is
administered. A case man-
ager is assigned to monitor
treatment progress.

Diagram visualizing the idea of a four step program to restore a patient from acute depression to normalcy. From a National Medical Enterprises Inc. annual report.
ナショナルメディカル・エンタープライズ社のアニュアルリポートより、患者を急性鬱状態から正常な状態へと回復させる4段階のプログラム概念を視覚化したチャート。

STATISTICAL
TABLES & GRAPHS

CHARTS & SCORES

MAPS

ARCHITECTURAL
PLANS & DRAWINGS

INSTRUCTIONAL DIAGRAMS
FOR PRODUCTS

SCIENTIFIC
ILLUSTRATIONS

ROCHE PRODUCTS LIMITED
ENGLAND 1971
CD,AD,D:Mervyn Kurlansky
D:Maddy Bennet
DF:Pentagram Design Ltd.

ERICSSON INFORMATION SYSTEMS
ENGLAND 1983
CD,AD,D:David Hillman
D:Bruce Mau/Sarah Pyne
DF:Pentagram Design Ltd.

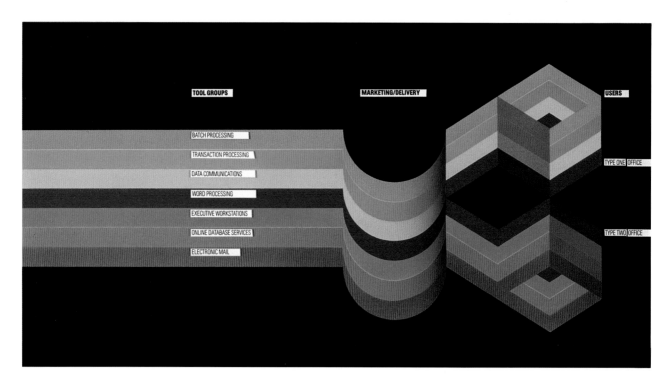

Illustration showing the main dimensions of personality.
From a Roche Products Limited promotional
brochure for a new tranquillizer.
ロッシュ・プロダクツ社の新精神安定剤のプロモーション用パンフレットより、人格の主な種類を示すチャート。

Color-coded chart showing the specific requirements of two types of offices.
From Information Resource Management magazine.
「インフォメーション・リソース・マネージメントマガジン」より、
オフィスが必要とする2タイプの特定の要素を色分けで示すチャート。

STATISTICAL
TABLES & GRAPHS

CHARTS & SCORES

MAPS

ARCHITECTURAL
PLANS & DRAWINGS

INSTRUCTIONAL DIAGRAMS
FOR PRODUCTS

SCIENTIFIC
ILLUSTRATIONS

ERICSSON INFORMATION SYSTEMS
ENGLAND 1983
CD,AD,D:David Hillman
D:Bruce Mau/Sarah Pyne
DF:Pentagram Design Ltd.

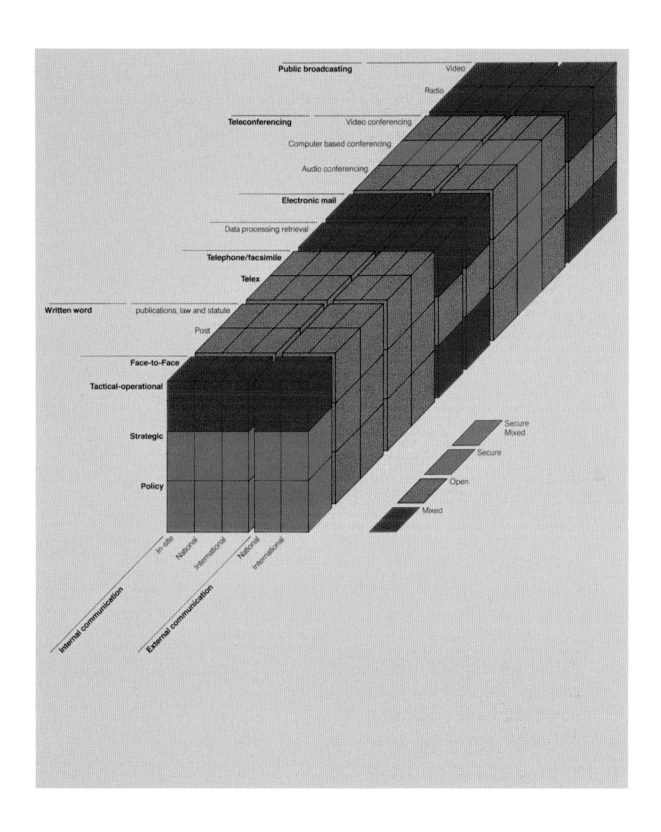

Chart showing communication within the company. From Information Resource Management magazine.
「インフォメーション・リソース・マネージメントマガジン」より、会社内でのコミュニケーションの様子を表すチャート。

STATISTICAL
TABLES & GRAPHS

CHARTS & SCORES

MAPS

ARCHITECTURAL
PLANS & DRAWINGS

INSTRUCTIONAL DIAGRAMS
FOR PRODUCTS

SCIENTIFIC
ILLUSTRATIONS

今日の会社組織におけるコンピューターの役割を表すチャート。

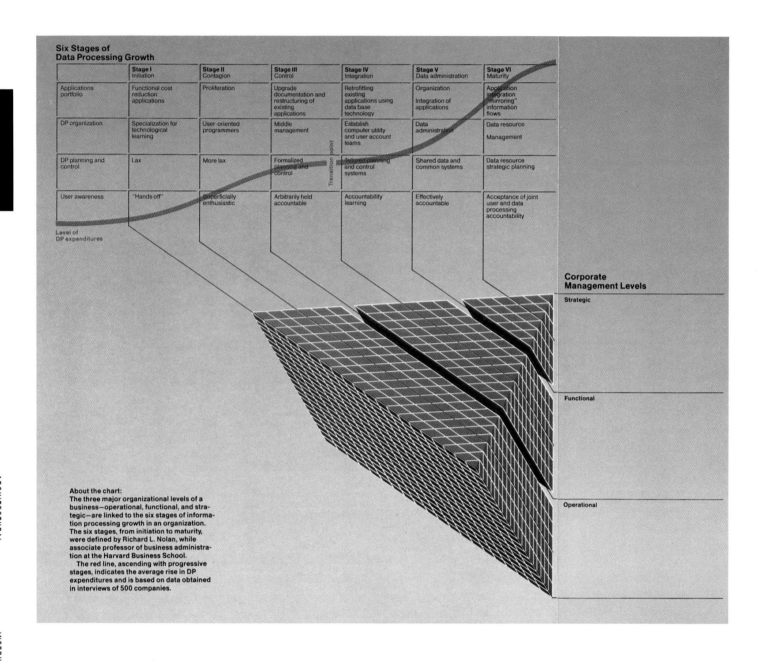

Six Stages of Data Processing Growth

	Stage I\nInitiation	Stage II\nContagion	Stage III\nControl	Stage IV\nIntegration	Stage V\nData administration	Stage VI\nMaturity
Applications portfolio	Functional cost reduction applications	Proliferation	Upgrade documentation and restructuring of existing applications	Retrofitting existing applications using data base technology	Organization\n\nIntegration of applications	Application integration "mirroring" information flows
DP organization	Specialization for technological learning	User-oriented programmers	Middle management	Establish computer utility and user account teams	Data administration	Data resource\n\nManagement
DP planning and control	Lax	More lax	Formalized planning and control	Tailored planning and control systems	Shared data and common systems	Data resource strategic planning
User awareness	"Hands off"	Superficially enthusiastic	Arbitrarily held accountable	Accountability learning	Effectively accountable	Acceptance of joint user and data processing accountability

Transition point

Level of DP expenditures

Corporate Management Levels

Strategic

Functional

Operational

About the chart:
The three major organizational levels of a business—operational, functional, and strategic—are linked to the six stages of information processing growth in an organization. The six stages, from initiation to maturity, were defined by Richard L. Nolan, while associate professor of business administration at the Harvard Business School.

The red line, ascending with progressive stages, indicates the average rise in DP expenditures and is based on data obtained in interviews of 500 companies.

Chart demonstrating the vertical pathways of computing in a contemporary corporation.
今日の会社組織におけるコンピューターの役割を表すチャート。

STATISTICAL
TABLES & GRAPHS

CHARTS & SCORES

MAPS

ARCHITECTURAL
PLANS & DRAWINGS

INSTRUCTIONAL DIAGRAMS
FOR PRODUCTS

SCIENTIFIC
ILLUSTRATIONS

ERICSSON INFORMATION SYSTEMS
ENGLAND 1983
CD,AD,D:David Hillman
D:Bruce Mau/Sarah Pyne
DF:Pentagram Design Ltd.

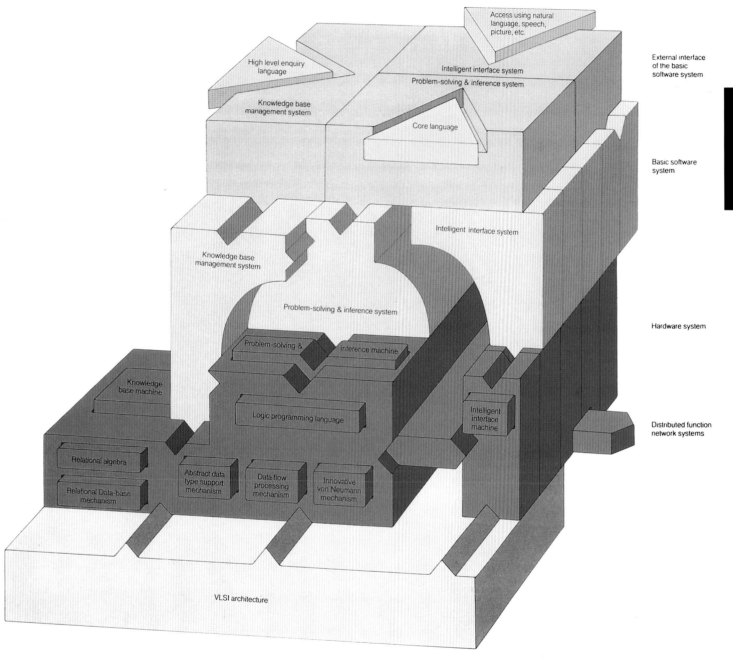

Basic configuration of the fifth generation computer systems. From Information Resource Management magazine.
「インフォメーション・リソース・マネージメントマガジン」より、第5世代コンピューターシステムの基本配置図。

STATISTICAL
TABLES & GRAPHS

CHARTS & SCORES

MAPS

ARCHITECTURAL
PLANS & DRAWINGS

INSTRUCTIONAL DIAGRAMS
FOR PRODUCTS

SCIENTIFIC
ILLUSTRATIONS

SEQUOIA SYSTEMS, INC.
USA 1991
AD:Stephen Mignogna
D:Victoria Stamm
I:In House
DF:Belk Mignogna Associates Ltd.

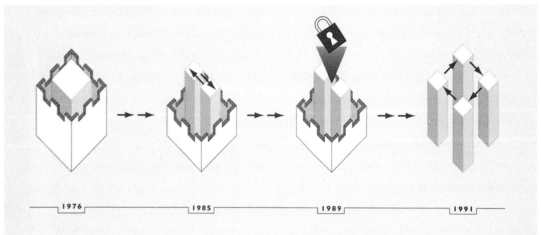

These charts illustrate Sequoia's dedication to serve its customer needs by focusing on technical strengths,
strategic alliances and service oriented capabilities. From a Sequoia Systems Inc. annual report.
セコイア・システムズ社のアニュアルリポートより、同社の技術力、戦略的提携、サービス能力を解説するチャート。

STATISTICAL
TABLES & GRAPHS

CHARTS & SCORES

MAPS

ARCHITECTURAL
PLANS & DRAWINGS

INSTRUCTIONAL DIAGRAMS
FOR PRODUCTS

SCIENTIFIC
ILLUSTRATIONS

JANNOCK LIMITED
CANADA 1992
AD,D:Roslyn Eskind
D:Sandi King
I:Gary Mansbridge
DF:Eskind Waddell

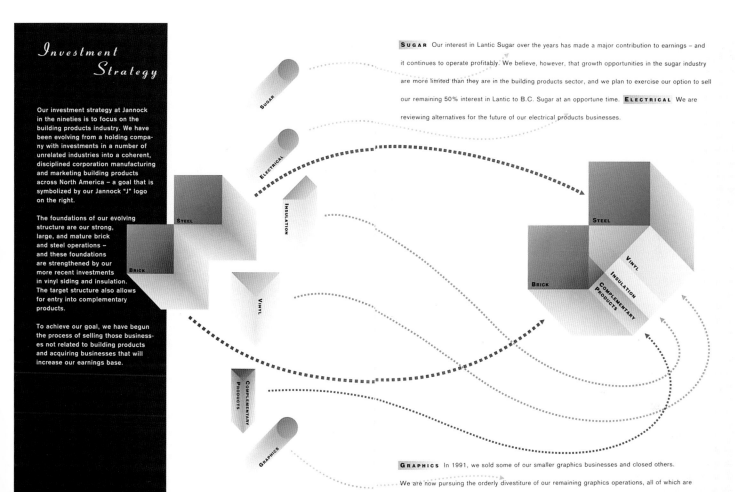

Investment Strategy

Our investment strategy at Jannock in the nineties is to focus on the building products industry. We have been evolving from a holding company with investments in a number of unrelated industries into a coherent, disciplined corporation manufacturing and marketing building products across North America – a goal that is symbolized by our Jannock "J" logo on the right.

The foundations of our evolving structure are our strong, large, and mature brick and steel operations – and these foundations are strengthened by our more recent investments in vinyl siding and insulation. The target structure also allows for entry into complementary products.

To achieve our goal, we have begun the process of selling those businesses not related to building products and acquiring businesses that will increase our earnings base.

SUGAR Our interest in Lantic Sugar over the years has made a major contribution to earnings – and it continues to operate profitably. We believe, however, that growth opportunities in the sugar industry are more limited than they are in the building products sector, and we plan to exercise our option to sell our remaining 50% interest in Lantic to B.C. Sugar at an opportune time. **ELECTRICAL** We are reviewing alternatives for the future of our electrical products businesses.

GRAPHICS In 1991, we sold some of our smaller graphics businesses and closed others. We are now pursuing the orderly divestiture of our remaining graphics operations, all of which are viable entities.

JANNOCK LIMITED 6

7 JANNOCK LIMITED

Chart illustrating strategic divestiture of unrelated businesses, with the corporate symbol as a matrix. From a Jannock Limited annual report.
ジャノック社のアニュアルリポートより、企業のシンボルをモチーフに非関連事業の戦略的な獲得のしくみを表すチャート。

STATISTICAL
TABLES & GRAPHS

CHARTS & SCORES

MAPS

ARCHITECTURAL
PLANS & DRAWINGS

INSTRUCTIONAL DIAGRAMS
FOR PRODUCTS

SCIENTIFIC
ILLUSTRATIONS

AGOURON PHARMACEUTICALS, INC.
USA 1989
AD,D:Rik Besser
AD:Douglas Joseph
P:Jeff Zaruba
DF:Besser Joseph Partners, Inc.

A crystallographer monitors experiments within multiple-well dishes. Each well contains a drop of the target protein in different solvents, which may produce protein crystals to be used in x-ray diffraction studies.

CLONING

CRYSTALLIZATION

STRUCTURE DETERMINATION

Scientists experiment with solubilized target protein under a variety of conditions to obtain diffraction quality crystals of the target protein.

DRUG DESIGN

SYNTHESIS

BIOEVALUATION

Chart displaying all steps necessary for protein structure-based drug design. From an Agouron Pharmaceuticals Inc. annual report.
アグーロン製薬会社のアニュアルリポートより、蛋白質構造をモチーフに薬品開発に必要なすべての段階を表したチャート。

STATISTICAL
TABLES & GRAPHS

CHARTS & SCORES

MAPS

ARCHITECTURAL
PLANS & DRAWINGS

INSTRUCTIONAL DIAGRAMS
FOR PRODUCTS

SCIENTIFIC
ILLUSTRATIONS

APPLIED BIOSYSTEMS INC.
USA 1991
CD,AD:Michael J. Zinke
D,I:Lesley Gasparetti
DF:Bay Graphics Design, Inc.

Charts showing steps in preparing DNA sample for one-lane sequencing by pairing four primers, labeled with flourescent dyes, with specific dideoxynucleotide reactions.
From an Applied Biosystems Inc. sales brochure.
アプライド・バイオシステムズ社の製品パンフレットより、ディオキシヌクレオチド反応のある4つの核分子を組み合わせてワンレーンシーケンス用のDNAサンプルを作成する段階図。

UNA
NETHERLANDS 1988
AD:Hans Bockting/
Will de l'Ecluse
AD,D,P:Henk Hoebë
P:Pieter Vandermeer
DF:UNA Amsterdam

STATISTICAL
TABLES & GRAPHS

CHARTS & SCORES

MAPS

ARCHITECTURAL
PLANS & DRAWINGS

INSTRUCTIONAL DIAGRAMS
FOR PRODUCTS

SCIENTIFIC
ILLUSTRATIONS

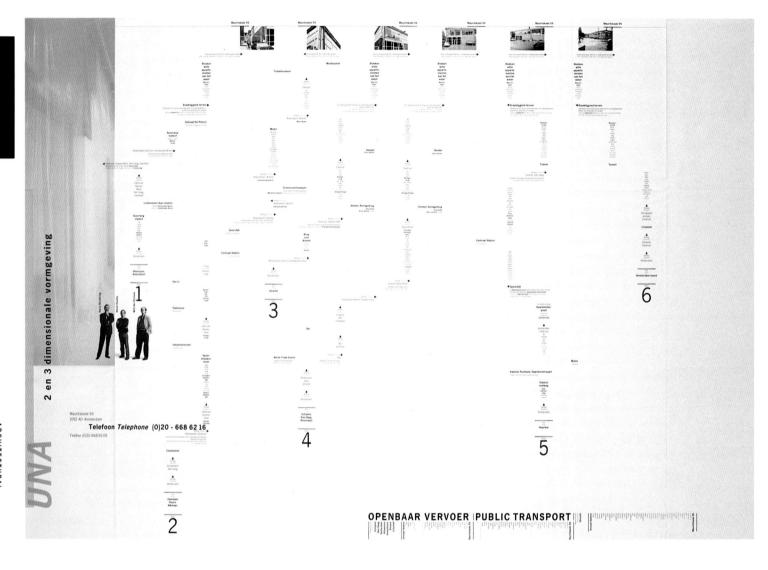

Chart of directions for reaching UNA Amsterdam's new offices (from six different starting points).
Each set of instructions is laid out in the direction of travel across a fold-out sheet.
デザイン会社「UNAアムステルダム」の新オフィスへの行き方を示すチャート。6つの異なった出発地点からそれぞれの行き方が説明されている。

STATISTICAL
TABLES & GRAPHS

CHARTS & SCORES

MAPS

ARCHITECTURAL
PLANS & DRAWINGS

INSTRUCTIONAL DIAGRAMS
FOR PRODUCTS

SCIENTIFIC
ILLUSTRATIONS

System tree for Nippon Electric Glass' high-tech glass products.

日本電気硝子社のハイテクガラス製品の系統樹。

STATISTICAL
TABLES & GRAPHS

CHARTS & SCORES

MAPS

ARCHITECTURAL
PLANS & DRAWINGS

INSTRUCTIONAL DIAGRAMS
FOR PRODUCTS

SCIENTIFIC
ILLUSTRATIONS

COLLAGEN CORPORATION
USA 1991
CD,AD,D,I:Earl Gee
D:Fani Chung
DF:Earl Gee Design

Symbolic flowchart highlighting the company's objectives and direction. The gradated boxes symbolize the company's transition. From a Collagen Corporation annual report.
コラーゲン社のアニュアルリポートより。会社の目標、及び方向性に焦点を当てたフローチャート。四角の中のグラデーションは会社の変遷を象徴している。

Concept Behind The Building

麻布十番の将来のあり方 Realizing the Potential of Azabu Ju-ban

東京の新ZONE TOKYO'S NEWEST ZONE

オリジナリティの発揮的拡大化
衣食住創造のクロスオーバー
各種レベルでの国際化
六本木との差別化

An expansion of opportunities for creative expression.
An overlapping of sustenance, shelter, fashion, creativity and play.
Internationalization on a day-to-day level.
Well defined character vis-a-vis Roppongi.

時代状況 Factors of the Times

仕事・生活・遊びの境界の曖昧化
仕事・生活・遊びの空間接近
国際化・感性化の進行

Increasingly vague demarcation between work, play, and day-to-day living.
Overlapping of work, play and living environments.
Internationalization and increasing sense of aesthetics.

マーケット トレンド Market Trends

本物+α

Authenticity + added value.

麻布十番の地域特性 Azabu Ju-ban Community Characteristics

<3要素>
伝統的東京の下町
首位性の国際性
CITYとしての器

<Indispensables>
A traditional Tokyo downtown neighborhood.
A casual, international atmosphere.
Sophisticated URBAN infrastructure.

JOULE-A'S TOTAL CONCEPT
共存と融合 SYNERGY AND FUSION

都市エネルギーの発信拠点 The Focal Point for New Explosion of Urban Energy

異なった感性を持つ人々の共有空間
テンションとリラクゼーションの共存
衣食住創造空間の共存
機能性と快適性の共存

A communal space which appeals to a variety of aesthetics.
Tension and Relaxation.
Sustenance, Shelter, Fashion, Creativity and Play.
Efficiency and Comfort.

麻布十番のシンボル A Symbol for Azabu Ju-ban

従来の魅力を集約したシンボル
中心・中立の地の活性化の核
ランドマークとしての集客効果
将来の力の象徴の表現

Emphasizing the attractive aspects of the neighborhood.
A nucleus of vitality in a sprawling, unfocused area.
The drawing-power of a landmark.
A symbolic expression of area potential.

建築アイデア Architectural Theme

二重性の表現 LAYERED EXPRESSION
ANARCHITECTURE

ハイテク/ロジー	ハイタッチ
徹底したインテリジェント化	快適と安らぎの追求
FULL METAL JAKCET	開放性
モノトーンのファサード	内部空間のやさしさ
	内部に配された豊かな緑

Advanced technology.	High Sense.
Fully intelligent building.	An emphasis on comfort and relaxation.
Sheltered.	Openness.
Full Metal Jacket.	Intimate spaces.
Monotone facade.	Abundant interior greenery.

Naming Concept

異種の共存、また融合はいつの時代にもパワーを作り出します。血は混じりありうことによってより強いもの、よりすぐれたものを生みだすのです。麻布十番が持つ魅力はまさにここにあるといってよいでしょう。異質な人々が、異質な感性を持って1つのユニークな文化を作り出しているのです。

そしてそこにこれからの都市のあり方があります。

都市が異質なものの共存によってその都市エネルギーをうみだしているのなら、そこに建てられる建築物は、都市エネルギーの発信拠点であるべきです。

こうしてジュールAのネイミングはなされました。

JOULE(ジュール)はENERGYの単位です。

1つの単位から発信されたENER-GYが、街を、都市を大きく発展させ、またそこに生きる人々を豊かにするような、そんな街づくりのスタートでありたい。

AはAZABUのAです。

そしてまた、スタートのAでもあるのです。

Synergy and fusion have been recognized as sources of power throughout the ages.
A mingling of bloodlines leads to the emergence of a better, stronger generation, of leaders for a new and vigorous future.
Such is the appeal of Azabu Ju-ban, a neighborhood where a variety of people embracing a diverse aesthetic have created a singularly unique culture.

Here is a glimpse of the city of the future.

A uniquely urban energy is born through the synergy of coexisting elements: the structures of the cityscape ideally serve as focal points for the explosion of urban energy.

So evolved the name, "JOULE A."

A "JOULE" is a unit of energy.
Energy to revitalize a neighborhood or an entire city, energy contributing to the prosperity of those who make the city their home.
Such a single unit of energy can become the catalyst for a whole new style of urban living.

"A"—the first letter in "Azabu."

"A"—the symbol of a new starting point. . . .

STATISTICAL
TABLES & GRAPHS

CHARTS & SCORES

MAPS

ARCHITECTURAL
PLANS & DRAWINGS

INSTRUCTIONAL DIAGRAMS
FOR PRODUCTS

SCIENTIFIC
ILLUSTRATIONS

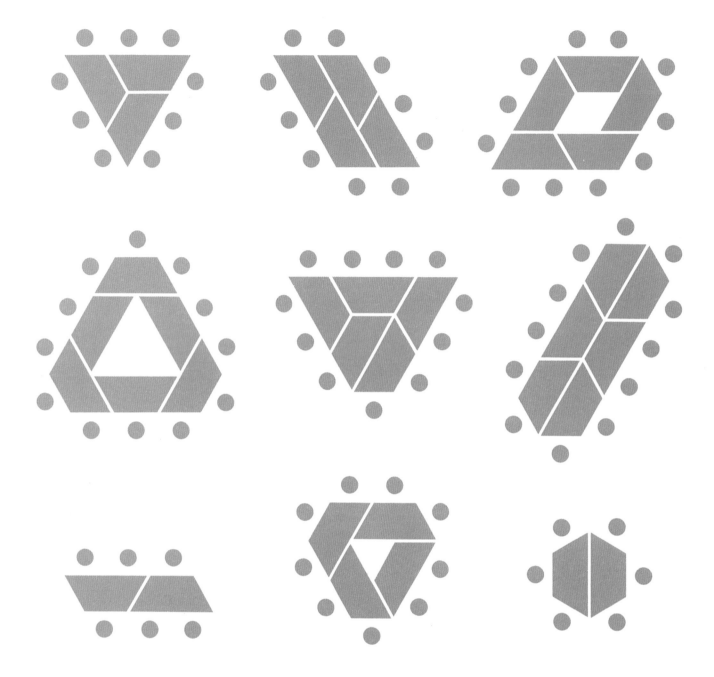

A single modular element is the basis for at least nine different table layouts for meetings. The dots represent the clients and executives of the advertising agency.
少なくとも9通りはある会議用のテーブル・レイアウト図。一つのモジュールが基本の構成要素となり、点はクライアントと広告代理店の幹部を表す。

VISCOM LTD.
ENGLAND 1979
CD,AD,D:David Hillman
D:Nancy Williams/Liz James
I:Dan Fern
DF:Pentagram Design Ltd.

STATISTICAL
TABLES & GRAPHS

CHARTS & SCORES

MAPS

ARCHITECTURAL
PLANS & DRAWINGS

INSTRUCTIONAL DIAGRAMS
FOR PRODUCTS

SCIENTIFIC
ILLUSTRATIONS

A symbol for a visual communications company involved in film-making
- the basic semaphore figure is used to spell out the name of film trailers in both animation and print forms.
映画制作に関わるビジュアル・コミュニケーション会社のシンボル。基本的な手旗信号はアニメーションや印刷物において、映画予告を表すために使用されている。

STATISTICAL
TABLES & GRAPHS

CHARTS & SCORES

MAPS

ARCHITECTURAL
PLANS & DRAWINGS

INSTRUCTIONAL DIAGRAMS
FOR PRODUCTS

SCIENTIFIC
ILLUSTRATIONS

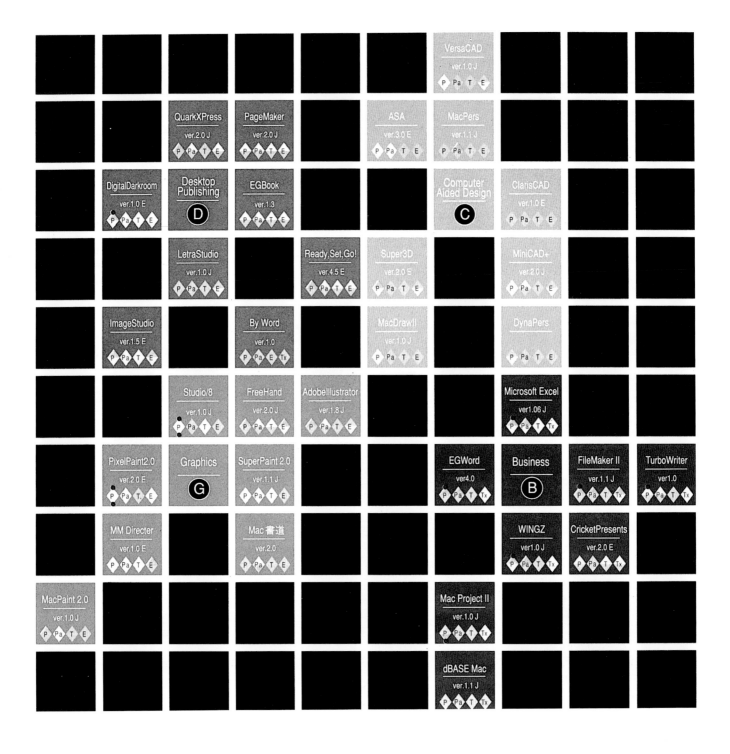

Pictograph indicating the functions of various software programs for the Macintosh computer.
マッキントッシュ・コンピューターの各ソフトの機能をピクトグラムで表したチャート。

YAMATO INTERNATIONAL INC.
JAPAN 1991
CD:Junichi Itoh
AD,D:Mari Sasaki

Shareholders' Meeting

Board of Directors

Auditors

President

Administrative Headquarters

Business Headquarters

Osaka Head Office

Tokyo Head Office

International Headquarters

Secretariat

Corporate Planning Office

Internal Auditing Office

Personnel Division

General Affairs Division

Accounting Division

Systems Division

Distribution and Warehousing Division

Merchandise Product Development and Technology Division

Marketing Division

Production Control Division

Ishikiri Factory

Wakayama Factory

Business Division I

Business Division II

Business Division III

Business Division V

Business Division VI

Business Division VII

Business Division XI

Department Store Section

Fukuoka Office

Nagoya Office

Tokyo Business Division I

Tokyo Business Division V

Tokyo Business Division VI

Tokyo Business Division VII

Business Division VIII

Business Division X

Business Division II Tokyo Sales Section

Business Division III Tokyo Sales Section

Business Division XI Tokyo Sales Section

Tokyo Department Store Division

Overseas Trade Division

Overseas Planning Department

STATISTICAL TABLES & GRAPHS

CHARTS & SCORES

MAPS

ARCHITECTURAL PLANS & DRAWINGS

INSTRUCTIONAL DIAGRAMS FOR PRODUCTS

SCIENTIFIC ILLUSTRATIONS

Corporate organizational diagram. From a Yamato International Inc. annual report.
ヤマト・インターナショナル社のアニュアルリポートより、会社組織図。

STATISTICAL
TABLES & GRAPHS

CHARTS & SCORES

MAPS

ARCHITECTURAL
PLANS & DRAWINGS

INSTRUCTIONAL DIAGRAMS
FOR PRODUCTS

SCIENTIFIC
ILLUSTRATIONS

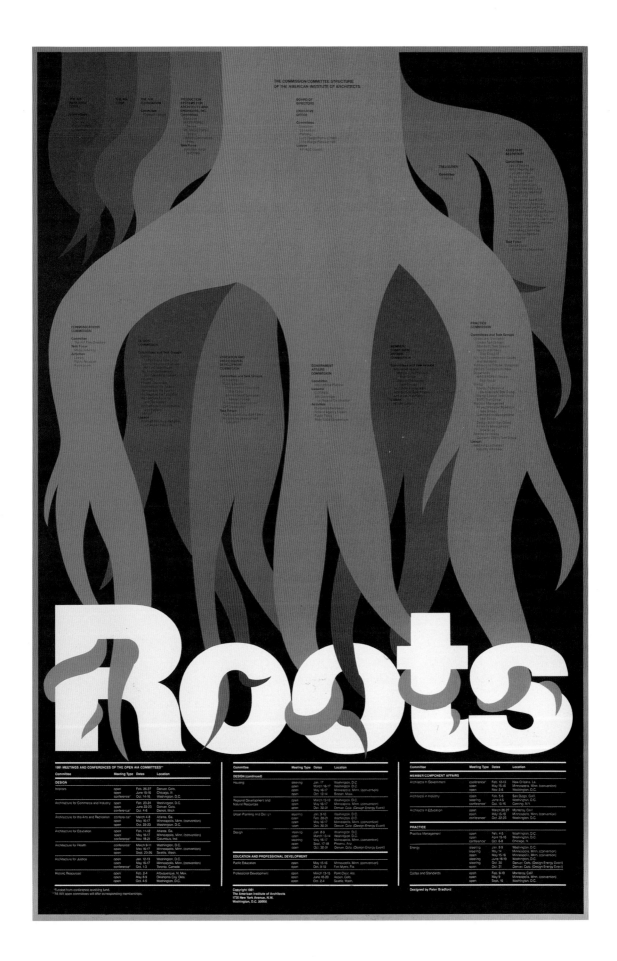

Chart of AIA's organizational structure and schedule of regional events.
AIA（アメリカ建築家協会）の組織の構造を表した図と諸地域で開催されるイベントのスケジュール表。

ASPEN DESIGN CONFERENCE
USA
AD,D,I:Peter Bradford
AD:Richard Saul Wurman
DF:Peter Bradford & Associates

STATISTICAL
TABLES & GRAPHS

CHARTS & SCORES

MAPS

ARCHITECTURAL
PLANS & DRAWINGS

INSTRUCTIONAL DIAGRAMS
FOR PRODUCTS

SCIENTIFIC
ILLUSTRATIONS

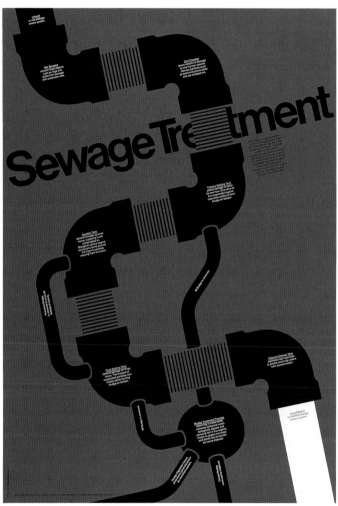

Diagrams of an underground utility system and typical city sewage treatment system.
地下を利用する公共事業設備、及び典型的な都市の下水処理システムを表したダイアグラム。

STATISTICAL
TABLES & GRAPHS

CHARTS & SCORES

MAPS

ARCHITECTURAL
PLANS & DRAWINGS

INSTRUCTIONAL DIAGRAMS
FOR PRODUCTS

SCIENTIFIC
ILLUSTRATIONS

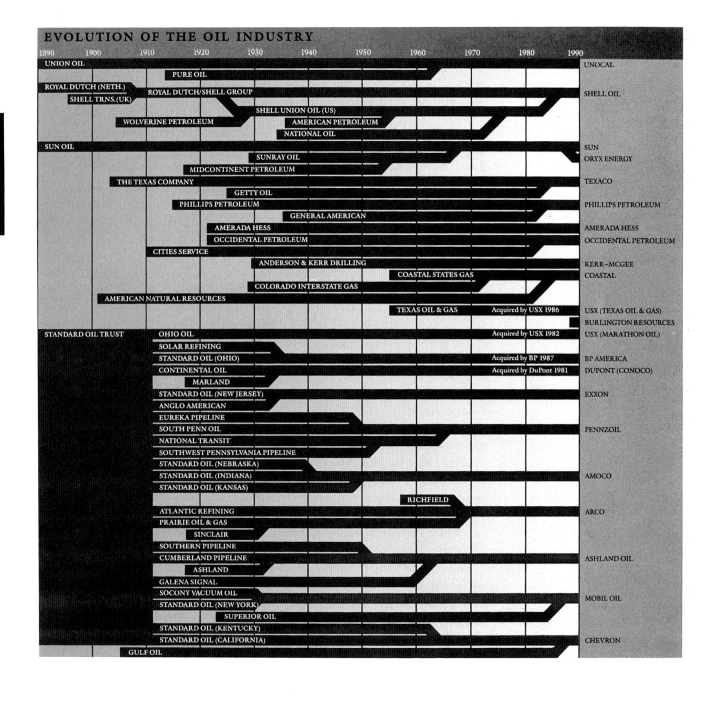

EVOLUTION OF THE OIL INDUSTRY

| 1890 | 1900 | 1910 | 1920 | 1930 | 1940 | 1950 | 1960 | 1970 | 1980 | 1990 |

UNION OIL — UNOCAL
PURE OIL
ROYAL DUTCH (NETH.)
SHELL TRNS.(UK) — ROYAL DUTCH/SHELL GROUP — SHELL OIL
SHELL UNION OIL (US)
WOLVERINE PETROLEUM — AMERICAN PETROLEUM
NATIONAL OIL
SUN OIL — SUN
SUNRAY OIL — ORYX ENERGY
MIDCONTINENT PETROLEUM
THE TEXAS COMPANY — TEXACO
GETTY OIL
PHILLIPS PETROLEUM — PHILLIPS PETROLEUM
GENERAL AMERICAN
AMERADA HESS — AMERADA HESS
OCCIDENTAL PETROLEUM — OCCIDENTAL PETROLEUM
CITIES SERVICE
ANDERSON & KERR DRILLING — KERR–MCGEE
COASTAL STATES GAS — COASTAL
COLORADO INTERSTATE GAS
AMERICAN NATURAL RESOURCES
TEXAS OIL & GAS — Acquired by USX 1986 — USX (TEXAS OIL & GAS)
BURLINGTON RESOURCES
STANDARD OIL TRUST — OHIO OIL — Acquired by USX 1982 — USX (MARATHON OIL)
SOLAR REFINING
STANDARD OIL (OHIO) — Acquired by BP 1987 — BP AMERICA
CONTINENTAL OIL — Acquired by DuPont 1981 — DUPONT (CONOCO)
MARLAND
STANDARD OIL (NEW JERSEY) — EXXON
ANGLO AMERICAN
EUREKA PIPELINE
SOUTH PENN OIL — PENNZOIL
NATIONAL TRANSIT
SOUTHWEST PENNSYLVANIA PIPELINE
STANDARD OIL (NEBRASKA)
STANDARD OIL (INDIANA) — AMOCO
STANDARD OIL (KANSAS)
RICHFIELD
ATLANTIC REFINING — ARCO
PRAIRIE OIL & GAS
SINCLAIR
SOUTHERN PIPELINE
CUMBERLAND PIPELINE — ASHLAND OIL
ASHLAND
GALENA SIGNAL
SOCONY VACUUM OIL
STANDARD OIL (NEW YORK) — MOBIL OIL
SUPERIOR OIL
STANDARD OIL (KENTUCKY)
STANDARD OIL (CALIFORNIA) — CHEVRON
GULF OIL

Chart describing how oil is produced. From a Unocal Corporation history book.
ユノカル社の社史より、石油の生産方法を解説したチャート。

PFU LTD.

JAPAN 1991

D:Yukimasa Matsuda

SEARS ROEBUCK & CO.

USA 1989

AD:Robert Gersin

D:David Au

I:Alan Kikuchi

DF:Robert P. Gersin Assoc. Inc.

CHARTS & SCORES

MAPS

ARCHITECTURAL
PLANS & DRAWINGS

INSTRUCTIONAL DIAGRAMS
FOR PRODUCTS

SCIENTIFIC
ILLUSTRATIONS

Packaging Procedure Model
The Sears Packaging Design System helps to clarify and streamline the decision-making process. It creates an organizational framework of procedures and guidelines that result in a more productive and efficient use of time.

Reductions in time translate into cost savings.

The Procedure Model shows the seven discrete phases in the life of a package. In this illustration phases are shown in linear form although the process is in reality a cycle incorporating a

feedback mechanism. As a package becomes obsolete a new package is created using feedback from the obsolete package to increase the effectiveness of the new package design.

Phases 1, 2 and 3
This manual is concerned only with phase 1. Planning, 2. Design & Development, and 3. Production.

These first three phases clarify the decision-making process and the procedures involved in designing

and producing a package. The three phases establish a structure of tasks, responsibilities and authorizations from planning to production. This structure can be used to achieve repeatable speed, economy, quality and appropriateness in packaging design and production.

Phases 4, 5 and 6
Phases 4. Distribution, 5. In-store Stock Keeping, and 6. End Use are concerned with the use of the package from initial storage through transportation, in-store merchandising and customer purchase.

Phase 7
In phase 7. Obsolescence, the package is considered obsolete and an evaluation of its effectiveness is made before a new package is designed and the cycle begins again.

Diagram of the history of information and communication over the past 30 years.
過去30年間の情報とコミュニケーションの歴史を解説したチャート。

Chart illustrating package lifetime
from identification of need through design and production to obsolescence.
需要を確認し、デザイン、生産、やがては使用廃止に至るまでのパッケージの終生を解説するチャート。

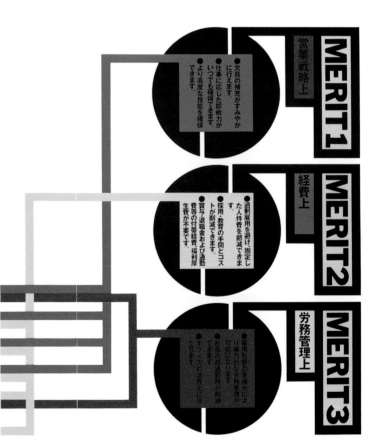

STATISTICAL
TABLES & GRAPHS

CHARTS & SCORES

MAPS

ARCHITECTURAL
PLANS & DRAWINGS

INSTRUCTIONAL DIAGRAMS
FOR PRODUCTS

SCIENTIFIC
ILLUSTRATIONS

1. N.I STAFF CORPORATION

JAPAN 1988

AD,D:Osamu Sato

2. THE KOMATSU STORE CO., LTD.

JAPAN 1988

AD,D:Ichiro Higashiizumi

D:Kazuhiro Kishi

DF:Huia Media Design Co., Ltd.

1. Chart explaining the operations system of a personnel dispatching company.
From N.I Staff Corporation corporate introductions.

エヌアイ・スタッフ社の企業案内より、人材派遣会社の業務システムを説明するチャート。

2. Flow-chart type self analysis test for the Komatsu Store Co., Ltd. promotional brochure.

コマツ・ストアーのプロモーション用パンフレットより、自己診断テストのためのフローチャート。

STATISTICAL
TABLES & GRAPHS

CHARTS & SCORES

MAPS

ARCHITECTURAL
PLANS & DRAWINGS

INSTRUCTIONAL DIAGRAMS
FOR PRODUCTS

SCIENTIFIC
ILLUSTRATIONS

3. XYPLEX, INC.
USA 1992
AD:Kathleen Forsythe
D:Renate Gokl
DF:Forsythe Design

3. Diagram of various local and remote office computer connectivity solutions provided by Xyplex equipment. From a Xyplex Inc. brochure.
サイフレックス社のパンフレットより、遠距離・近距離オフィス間のコンピュータ接続における問題に対し、同社が提供する各種の解決策を表すチャート。

STATISTICAL
TABLES & GRAPHS

CHARTS & SCORES

MAPS

ARCHITECTURAL
PLANS & DRAWINGS

INSTRUCTIONAL DIAGRAMS
FOR PRODUCTS

SCIENTIFIC
ILLUSTRATIONS

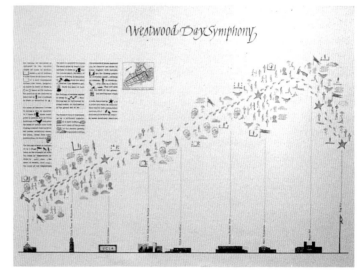

A score representing the activity on Westwood St., L.A. done separately for day and night.
ロサンジェルス/ウェストウッド通りの様子を昼夜別に記録、表現したスコア。

STATISTICAL
TABLES & GRAPHS

CHARTS & SCORES

MAPS

ARCHITECTURAL
PLANS & DRAWINGS

INSTRUCTIONAL DIAGRAMS
FOR PRODUCTS

SCIENTIFIC
ILLUSTRATIONS

Illustration showing a corporate-wide solution for electronic publishing. It runs on a range of computing hardware,
connects every department and produces a variety of documents. From an Interleaf Inc. annual report.

インターリーフ社のアニュアルリポートより、コンピューター・ネットワークの利用により、各部署が様々な文書を同時に出力することが可能な電子出版システムの利点を示すチャート。

STATISTICAL
TABLES & GRAPHS

CHARTS & SCORES

MAPS

ARCHITECTURAL
PLANS & DRAWINGS

INSTRUCTIONAL DIAGRAMS
FOR PRODUCTS

SCIENTIFIC
ILLUSTRATIONS

PFU LTD.

JAPAN 1990,1991

D:Yukimasa Matsuda

Storyline-scores of the movies, "Hitchcock's Rope", "Alien" and "Back to the Future". From the PFU Ltd. promotional brochure "Banbutsuzukan".

PFU社のプロモーション用パンフレット「万物図鑑」より、映画「ヒチコックのロープ」「エイリアン」「バックトゥザフューチャー」のストーリーをグラフィックで説明したスコア。

PFU LTD.
JAPAN 1990
D:Yukimasa Matsuda

STATISTICAL TABLES & GRAPHS

CHARTS & SCORES

MAPS

ARCHITECTURAL PLANS & DRAWINGS

INSTRUCTIONAL DIAGRAMS FOR PRODUCTS

SCIENTIFIC ILLUSTRATIONS

Chart of the victims in the movie, "Friday the 13th". From the PFU Ltd. promotional brochure "Banbutsuzukan".
PFU社のプロモーション用パンフレット「万物図鑑」より、映画「13日の金曜日」の犠牲者たちの状況をグラフィックで表現したチャート。

BNN CO.
JAPAN 1990
CD:Shoji Otsuki
AD,D,I:Mitsunobu Murakami

STATISTICAL
TABLES & GRAPHS

CHARTS & SCORES

MAPS

ARCHITECTURAL
PLANS & DRAWINGS

INSTRUCTIONAL DIAGRAMS
FOR PRODUCTS

SCIENTIFIC
ILLUSTRATIONS

System diagram for software programs for the Macintosh computer. From Maclife magazine.
月刊誌「マックライフ」より、マッキントッシュ・コンピューターのソフト系統図。

BNN CO.

JAPAN 1991

AD,D:Sonoe Takigami

STATISTICAL
TABLES & GRAPHS

CHARTS & SCORES

MAPS

ARCHITECTURAL
PLANS & DRAWINGS

INSTRUCTIONAL DIAGRAMS
FOR PRODUCTS

SCIENTIFIC
ILLUSTRATIONS

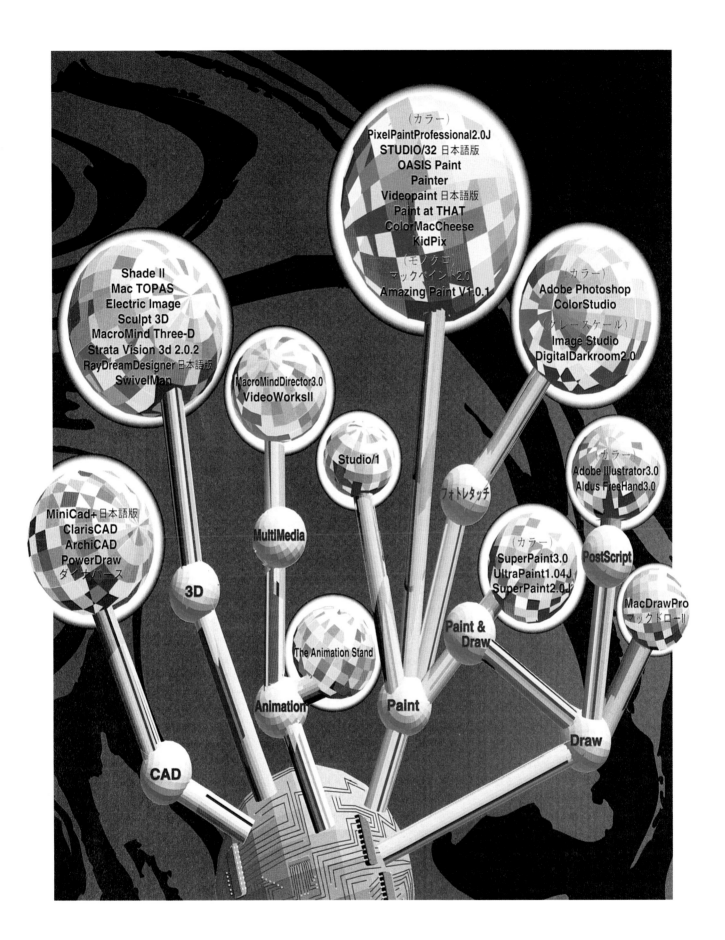

Genealogical tree of graphics software programs for the Macintosh computer. From Maclife magazine.
月刊誌「マックライフ」より、マッキントッシュ・コンピューターのグラフィックソフト系譜図。

BOEHRINGER MANNHEIM CORPORATION
USA 1991
AD:Chris Gilbert
AD,D,I:Rebecca Simms
DF:Henry Dreyfuss Associates

STATISTICAL
TABLES & GRAPHS

CHARTS & SCORES

MAPS

ARCHITECTURAL
PLANS & DRAWINGS

INSTRUCTIONAL DIAGRAMS
FOR PRODUCTS

SCIENTIFIC
ILLUSTRATIONS

Graphic representations of the technology of three different methods of glucose self-monitoring for diabetic patients.
糖尿病患者が血糖を自己測定するための3つの方法における科学技術を解説するイラストレーション。

STATISTICAL
TABLES & GRAPHS

CHARTS & SCORES

MAPS

ARCHITECTURAL
PLANS & DRAWINGS

INSTRUCTIONAL DIAGRAMS
FOR PRODUCTS

SCIENTIFIC
ILLUSTRATIONS

BRITISH COUNCIL
ENGLAND 1986
CD:Richard Moon
D,I:Peter Grundy/Tilly Northedge
DF:Grundy & Northedge

MICHAEL PEHES LIHEAHVE
ENGLAND 1987
CD:Michael Peters
D,I:Peter Grundy/Tilly Northedge
DF:Grundy & Northedge

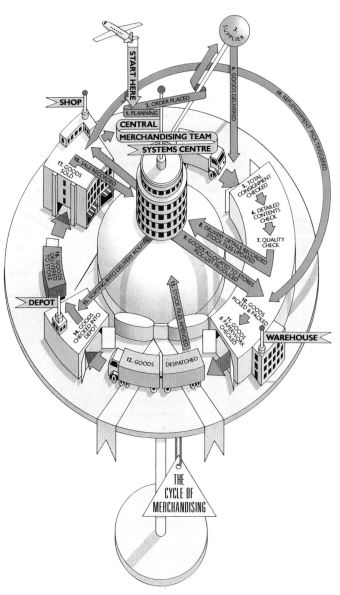

Structural diagram of the British Council's organization from an annual report.
ブリティッシュ・カウンシルのアニュアルリポートより、協会組織図。

Clothing distribution diagram for Burton. From an annual report.
バートン社のアニュアルリポートより、衣類流通経路図。

Diagram showing how they work with clients. From a Grundy & Northedge design firm promotional brochure.
デザイン会社「グランディ ＆ ノースエッジ」の宣伝用パンフレットより、顧客への応対の仕方を表しているチャート。

STATISTICAL TABLES & GRAPHS

CHARTS & SCORES

MAPS

ARCHITECTURAL PLANS & DRAWINGS

INSTRUCTIONAL DIAGRAMS FOR PRODUCTS

SCIENTIFIC ILLUSTRATIONS

STATISTICAL
TABLES & GRAPHS

CHARTS & SCORES

MAPS

ARCHITECTURAL
PLANS & DRAWINGS

INSTRUCTIONAL DIAGRAMS
FOR PRODUCTS

SCIENTIFIC
ILLUSTRATIONS

HILLHAVEN CORPORATION
USA 1991
AD,D:Jack Anderson
D:Mary Hermes
I:Jonathan Combs
DF:Hornall Anderson Design Works

ASDA
ENGLAND 1988,1989
AD,D:Amanda Tatham
I:Benoit Jacoues
DF:Tatham Pearce Ltd.

Chart dealing with long-term caregiving
from Hillhaven Corporation's brochure and poster.
ヒルヘイブン社のパンフレットやポスターより、長期ケアの様子を示すチャート。

Chart showing the performance of supermarket chain Asda
Group from a financial report to employees.
スーパーマーケット・チェーン「アスダグループ」の従業員への会計報告をイラストレーションで表したチャート。

GARBAGE MAGAZINE
USA 1992
AD:Patrick Mitchell
D,I:Scott A. MacNeill

STATISTICAL
TABLES & GRAPHS

CHARTS & SCORES

MAPS

ARCHITECTURAL
PLANS & DRAWINGS

INSTRUCTIONAL DIAGRAMS
FOR PRODUCTS

SCIENTIFIC
ILLUSTRATIONS

UNPLUGGING ELECTROMAGNETIC POLLUTION

The thought that our appliances are out to get us is a sobering one. Researchers continue to haggle over the dangers of electromagnetic radiation. In the meantime, we've taken an inventory of the electric-powered gadgets and gizmos that surround us. Every one, of course, is a source of pollution — CO_2 pollution from the power plant that runs them, plus the lifecycle pollution that every product generates when its materials are mined and processed, and when it eventually hits the landfill. And, of course, the "pollution" of electromagnetic fields, which we measure here in a typical suburban house. The Rocky Mountain Institute estimates there are 40 million electric garbage disposals, 80 million hair dryers, and 180 million electric clocks in this country, not to mention all the electric popcorn poppers, can openers, and weed whackers. Do we need them all?

The field strength is measured in milligauss. Some researchers feel more than 1 milligauss is dangerous, others think we needn't worry until the needle hits 2.5 or 3 mg. We used the Schaefer EM1 meter, which measures in ranges rather than specific numbers.

BATHROOM
Next to hair dryer:
ABOVE 10
Electric toothbrush:
7 to 10
Hand toothbrush:
0

LIVING ROOM
Stereo amplifier:
5 to 7
TV, at screen:
3.5 to 5
TV, at three feet:
.88 to 1.25

BEDROOM
Electric clock, at one foot:
1.8 to 2.5
Electric clock, at three feet:
.88 to 1.25
Hand-wound clock:
0
Under old electric blanket:
ABOVE 10
Under the cat:
0

KITCHEN
In front of electric stove:
5 to 7
In front of gas stove: **0**
Coffee grinder:
ABOVE 10
Toaster:
1.25 to 1.8

STUDY
Computer, at 12 inches:
2.5 to 3.5
Computer, at 24 inches:
1.25 to 1.8
Near the wall where the electric feed comes into the house:
ABOVE 10

OUTDOORS
In the car, at the dashboard:
ABOVE 10
In the car, at the front seat:
3.5 to 5
At the base of some electric poles:
7 to 10
Beneath wires at transformer station down the block:
ABOVE 10
At 50 feet away:
1.8 to 2.5

Graphics by Scott MacNEILL

38

39

Illustration showing the EMF ratings of various household electrical devices and their locations in the home.
各家電製品のEMF（起電力）値、及び家庭内配置図。

GROSSMONT HOSPITAL
USA 1992
CD:Monique Martineau
D,I:Tracy Sabin
DF:Sabin Design

STATISTICAL
TABLES & GRAPHS

CHARTS & SCORES

MAPS

ARCHITECTURAL
PLANS & DRAWINGS

INSTRUCTIONAL DIAGRAMS
FOR PRODUCTS

SCIENTIFIC
ILLUSTRATIONS

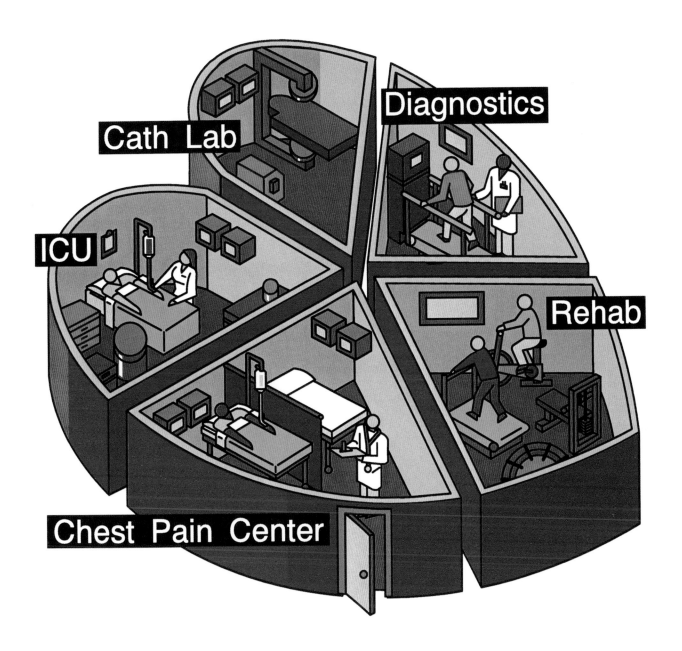

Chest Pain Center diagram used in newsletters and brochures.
ニュースレターやパンフレットに使用された「胸部ペインセンター」のチャート。

STATISTICAL
TABLES & GRAPHS

CHARTS & SCORES

MAPS

ARCHITECTURAL
PLANS & DRAWINGS

INSTRUCTIONAL DIAGRAMS
FOR PRODUCTS

SCIENTIFIC
ILLUSTRATIONS

THE FINE WHITE LINE
ENGLAND 1984
CD,AD:Siobhan Noonan
D,I:Tilly Northedge
DF:Grundy & Northedge Designers

Diagram showing how a car is assembled on a production line in as simple a way as possible. From a Vauxhall Motors Ltd. brochure.

ヴォークソール・モーターズ社のパンフレットより、自動車が組み立てられる様子を表した生産ライン図。

CENTOCOR, INC.
USA 1991
CD:Stephen Ferrari
D:John Ball
I:Michael Crumpton/
Martin Haggland/Micro Color
DF:The Graphic Expression, Inc.

DISCOVER
USA 1992
I:Andy Martin

STATISTICAL
TABLES & GRAPHS

CHARTS & SCORES

MAPS

ARCHITECTURAL
PLANS & DRAWINGS

INSTRUCTIONAL DIAGRAMS
FOR PRODUCTS

SCIENTIFIC
ILLUSTRATIONS

Production of Centoxin

Cell Propagation

1. CELL BANKS. Vials of antibody-producing cells used to make Centoxin are frozen in liquid nitrogen until production begins. The cell lines are tested to ensure stability and purity.

Antibody Production

4. BIOREACTOR. Through techniques developed by Centocor, the bioreactor continues to nourish a cell population that can grow to many billions and produce antibodies in large quantities.

5. FEED TANK. Nutrients and growth factors are pumped into the bioreactor at rates that keep antibody production at optimal levels.

6. CONTROL UNIT. Monitoring ensures proper temperature and pH and proper levels of nutrients, oxygen, and carbon dioxide.

7. HARVEST TANK. Antibodies, cellular debris, and extraneous fluids are removed from the bioreactor.

2. SMALL T-FLASK. After thawing, cells begin to multiply in the cell culture medium, a liquid mixture of nutrients and growth factors.

3. SPINNER FLASK. The culture medium is constantly stirred in order to bathe all the rapidly dividing cells. Once the population reaches requisite levels, the cells are delivered to a bioreactor.

Antibody Purification

8. DOWNSTREAM PROCESSING. Antibodies are separated from cell debris and other contaminants using methods devised by Centocor. Extensive testing demonstrates purity of the final product.

Vialing

9. STERILE FILLING LINE. The product is put into vials under sterile conditions, labeled, and packaged. Rigorous quality checks are performed on each production lot.

Centocor has pioneered the manufacture of human monoclonal antibodies in quantities sufficient to meet widespread clinical demand. ■ The production of Centoxin begins with a heterohybridoma, an immortal cell line capable of indefinitely secreting a specific human monoclonal antibody. Batches of the cell line are cultured, thoroughly tested for specificity, stability, and purity, then cryogenically stored until production begins. ■ Production techniques developed by Centocor allow it to make human monoclonal antibodies on a scale larger than that achieved by any other biopharmaceutical firm. Centoxin is being made initially in Centocor's 55,000-square-foot production plant in Leiden, Holland. Centocor recently agreed to purchase 90,000 square feet of facilities in St. Louis, including a modern, large-scale mammalian cell culture plant. Besides accelerating Centocor's plans to manufacture pharmaceuticals in both the United States and Europe, the acquisition gives the company additional innovative technology and experienced technical personnel. ■ Having plants in each of Centocor's most important markets offers the company flexibility in coordinating production with demand as well as assurance of an uninterrupted supply in case of fire or other disaster. ■ Centocor has invested more than $50 million in its manufacturing capacity and established itself as a pacesetter in making monoclonal antibodies a clinical and commercial reality. By retaining and protecting the cell-culture and purification techniques it has developed, the company keeps an important competitive edge.

10 11

Illustration of the manufacturing process for a new drug called Centoxin.
From a Centocor Inc. annual report.
セントコア社のアニュアルリポートより、新薬「セントキシン」の製造プロセスを表すイラストレーション。

Charts showing the effect of added road capacity on traffic delays.
From an article in Discover magazine.
「ディスカバー・マガジン」より、道路交通量の増加と通行の遅れとの関係を表したチャート。

STATISTICAL
TABLES & GRAPHS

CHARTS & SCORES

MAPS

ARCHITECTURAL
PLANS & DRAWINGS

INSTRUCTIONAL DIAGRAMS
FOR PRODUCTS

SCIENTIFIC
ILLUSTRATIONS

FIRST BOSTON
ASSET MANAGEMENT CORPORATION
USA
CD:Stephen Ferrari
I,DF:The Graphic Expression, Inc.

Chart showing the steps in customer/firm partnership used in
setting up an investment management program.
From a First Boston Asset Management Corporation brochure.
ファーストボストン・アセットマネージメント社のパンフレットより、
投資経営プログラムをたてるに際に使用される顧客と同社のパートナーシップの各段階を示すチャート。

UNOCAL CORPORATION
USA 1991
CD,AD,D,I:Ray Engle
DF:Ray Engle & Associates

STATISTICAL
TABLES & GRAPHS

CHARTS & SCORES

MAPS

ARCHITECTURAL
PLANS & DRAWINGS

INSTRUCTIONAL DIAGRAMS
FOR PRODUCTS

SCIENTIFIC
ILLUSTRATIONS

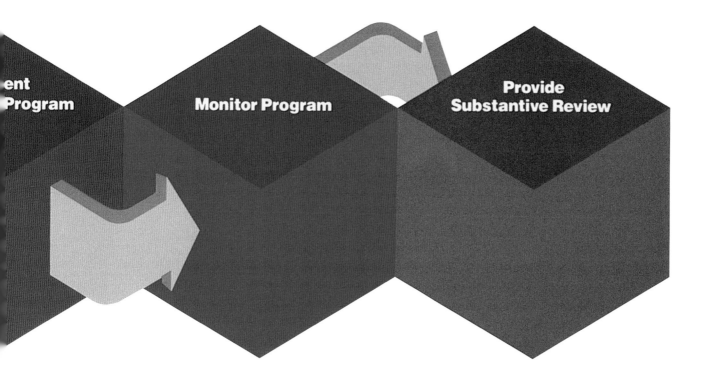

ent
Program

Monitor Program

**Provide
Substantive Review**

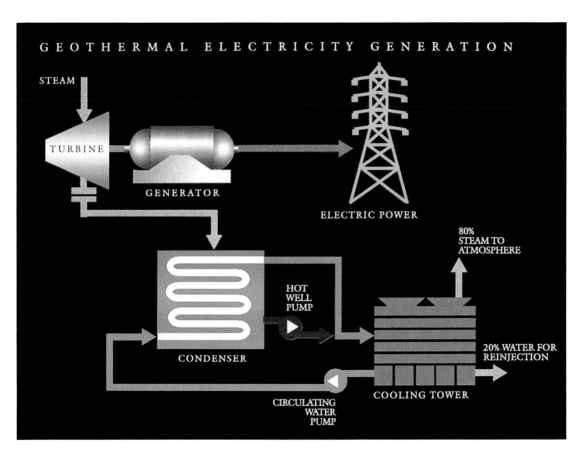

Chart of electricity generation for a magazine article on geothermal energy.
"地熱エネルギー"に関する雑誌記事より、発電のシステムを説明するチャート。

STATISTICAL TABLES & GRAPHS

CHARTS & SCORES

MAPS

ARCHITECTURAL PLANS & DRAWINGS

INSTRUCTIONAL DIAGRAMS FOR PRODUCTS

SCIENTIFIC ILLUSTRATIONS

ARCO
USA 1991
CD:Ron Jefferies
D:Scott Lambert
P:Keith Wood
I:Hank Fisher
DF:The Jefferies Association

"By committing capital expenditures totaling $1.8 billion for GHX-1 and GHX-2, the Prudhoe Bay partners increased production by 125,000 barrels a day at year-end 1990 and expect to further increase it by 100,000 barrels a day in 1993, with an expected increase in total recovery from both projects of over 800 million barrels. These projects and

other programs reflect ARCO's long-term commitment to the State of Alaska."

At Prudhoe Bay's separation facilities (1) crude oil is extracted and sent to the Trans Alaska Pipeline System (TAPS) while water is reinjected into the underground reservoir (4) and gas flows to the Central Gas Facility (CGF).

The Central Gas Facility (2) separates natural gas liquids (NGLs) and miscible gases from natural gas. NGLs are sent to TAPS and miscible gases are reinjected into the reservoir (4) for enhanced oil recovery.

High-quality assets and low-cost operations have been central to ARCO's competitive differentiation. Achievement of appropriate financial leverage is necessary to maintain our operating flexibility.

Each of ARCO's corporate strategies work in unison to build stockholder return. Paramount to these strategies has been concentration on the core hydrocarbons business, while integrating the best, most efficient use of capital markets to meet the Company's operating objectives.

Cameron Cooper Senior Vice President and Treasurer

"ARCO strives to be as competitive in the financial marketplace as it is in consumer markets. We intend to provide a quality 'product' which, in this instance, means that an investment in ARCO will provide a superior return over time. Our strategies have now been in

place for five years. They are focused on enhancing the returns from every aspect of our activities."

The natural gases enter the Central Compression Plant (3) before being returned to the reservoir (4) to increase liquid recovery and be available for potential future gas sales.

◆ Crude Oil

◆ Water

◆ Gas

◆ Natural Gas Liquids

◆ Miscible Gas

◆ Hydrocarbon-based

◆ Integration of capital markets

◆ High-quality assets, low costs

◆ Appropriate financial leverage

◆ Competitive differentiation

10   *33*

Diagram showing how crude oil is extracted from the reservoir and how miscible gases are reinjected and sent into the Trans Alaska Pipeline System (TAPS).
Diagram showing how five interconnecting strategies combine to build stockholder return. From an Arco annual report.
アルコ社のアニュアルリポートより、原油を貯蔵槽より引き出し、トランスアラスカ・パイプラインシステム（TAPS）に送る様子や混和性ガスを再注入する様子を表したチャート、
及び5つの相互に連結した戦略が株主の利益を築いていく様子を表したチャート。

STATISTICAL
TABLES & GRAPHS

CHARTS & SCORES

MAPS

ARCHITECTURAL
PLANS & DRAWINGS

INSTRUCTIONAL DIAGRAMS
FOR PRODUCTS

SCIENTIFIC
ILLUSTRATIONS

SIGMA XI
USA 1991
AD:Linda Huff
D:Michael Szpir
D,I:Elyse Carter

A computer-simulated insect reproduces some of the behaviors of the American cockroach.
The circuitry is color-coded for different aspects of the artificial insect's behavior. From American Scientist magazine.
「アメリカン・サイエンティストマガジン」より、人工昆虫を制作するためにコンピューターによりシミュレーションしたアメリカゴキブリの行動図。様々な行動の形態に従って回路が色分けされている。

STATISTICAL
TABLES & GRAPHS

CHARTS & SCORES

MAPS

ARCHITECTURAL
PLANS & DRAWINGS

INSTRUCTIONAL DIAGRAMS
FOR PRODUCTS

SCIENTIFIC
ILLUSTRATIONS

CHASE MANHATTEN BANK
ENGLAND 1985
CD,AD,D:Mervyn Kurlansky
D:Herman Lelie/Gillian Thomas
DF:Pentagram Design Ltd.

Chart explaining a marketing program for a bank.
銀行のマーケティングプログラムを説明したチャート。

マップ

マップすなわち地図は、私たちにとって最も身近なダイアグラムである。

基本的には、地域ないしは区域などの空間を表わすダイアグラムがマップである。私たちの生活は、空間を移動することによって成立しており、マップは、この空間の広がりと構造を図解することで、そこをいかに移動すれば目的の場所に着けるのかを私たちに教えてくれる。

言い換えるならば、空間と移動を結ぶダイアグラムがマップなのである。

ただし、たとえば「興味の範囲」、あるいは「業界の周辺」というように、私たちの日常の言葉の表現にも、厳密な意味では空間ではないものを空間的な比喩で表わす例も多く見られる。これがダイアグラムにも影響し、現実的な区域や空間ではないものを、比喩的に空間化してマップ化した作例も少なくはない。興味の地図、業界マップ・・・という具合いで、こうした作例においては、マップは単純に区域や地域と移動を結ぶダイアグラムではなく、むしろ、概念や現象の「空間」を探索するための教材として作用している。

こうした作例は、近年、特に増えており、ダイアグラム表現の一般化と成熟を反映すると共に、膨大な量の情報と多様なメディアに囲まれて生活する現代人が自然と身につけざるを得ない、柔軟かつ複合的な感受性をも裏書きしているといえよう。

自分の暮らす世界の中でのものの配置を記した「頭の中の地図」のことを、心理学では認知地図という。この認知地図は、言語の修得以前は幼児の頭の中でも成立しており、地図というものが、人間が世界を把握する上での最も基本的な感覚の図解であることが実感される。

それだけに、古来よりの作例も多く、手法的にも探求しつくされているのが、このマップというダイアグラムである。視覚的な機能をそこなわずに、なおかつ従来の伝統を超える新しいイメージは、マップにおいてはそう簡単に提示できるものではないだろう。

地球規模での情報ネットワークが完備し、世界が狭くなる分だけ、人間ひとりひとりの心が具体的に想起し得る空間が大きくなり続ける今日にあって、人々の空間イメージにどれだけ即応できるマップを作れるかは、デザイナーにとって大きな課題ではある。

MAPS

MAPS

マップ

Maps are the most familiar diagrams there are. Basically, a map is a diagram which indicates a region within boundaries. Since our lives proceed largely by moving from one place to another through space, a map, by illustrating the expanse and structure of that space, guides our movement so that we can reach our goals. In other words, a map is a diagram of the link between space and movement.

It is interesting to note the presence of such verbal expressions as "a wide range of interests" and "the peripheral areas of the industry " in our everyday speech. Here are things which are not, strictly speaking, spatial in nature, being expressed in language with spatial metaphors. A similar phenomenon can be seen in diagram making, where things which really have nothing to do with space are expressed metaphorically with space and are made into maps. In this case, a map is not merely a diagram that connects areas with vectors of movement. Here, it serves the usual function of text by operating as learning material. With such a map, one can explore the metaphorical space of concepts and phenomena. Examples of this sort of map have been increasing rapidly in recent years and this probably reflects the fact that diagrams, as a form of expression, have matured and become more generalized. It also reveals the flexible and complex sensitivity which modern people have had to acquire, surrounded as they are by vast quantities of information brought to them in a variety of media. In psychological terminology, "the map in your head," wherein the things of the outer world are arranged into the inner world in which you live, is called a cognitive map. This cognitive map is apparently present in the brain of even a very young child who has not yet acquired language. Thus, it is probably fair to conclude that a map is the most basic representation of the way in which human sensory data are organized in our attempts to understand the world around us.

It is not surprising to discover, then, that there exists a tremendous wealth of superb maps which date back to ancient times. In many cases, artistic techniques have reached their zenith in the production of maps. For the designer, of course, this means that it will not be easy to come up with a new approach or an original kind of image. It will be difficult to surpass what has already been done in mapping without downgrading its main purpose as a functional map.

Today, with global information networks being put in place, and the world getting smaller and smaller, the kind of space that can and must be contained in each person's mind is growing larger and larger. The map designer now has to tackle the considerable challenge of producing a map which corresponds closely to people's spatial images of the world.

**LONDON DOCKLANDS
DEVELOPMENT CORPORATION**
ENGLAND 1981
CD,AD,D:John McConnell
D:Kia Boon
DF:Pentagram Design Ltd.

STATISTICAL
TABLES & GRAPHS

CHARTS & SCORES

MAPS

ARCHITECTURAL
PLANS & DRAWINGS

FAWE STREET

EAST INDIA DOCK ROAD

NORTH QUAY

WEST FERRY ROAD

CANARY WHARF

LIMEHOUSE

HERON WHARF

BOW ROAD

DEVONS STREET

FAWE STREET

Figure showing tracks of the Docklands Light Railway, featuring the rail company's multipurpose sign system.
多目的サインシステムを取り入れている、ドッグランズライト鉄道の路線図。

STATISTICAL
TABLES & GRAPHS

CHARTS & SCORES

MAPS

ARCHITECTURAL
PLANS & DRAWINGS

INSTRUCTIONAL DIAGRAMS
FOR PRODUCTS

SCIENTIFIC
ILLUSTRATIONS

PENNSYLVANIA DEPARTMENT
OF TRANSPORTATION
USA 1991
CD:Lois Morasco
AD,D,I:Joel Katz
DF:Katz Wheeler Design

Guide to Interstate-476 providing information about the new expressway.
新しい高速道路「州間道路476号線」の情報ガイド。

STATISTICAL
TABLES & GRAPHS

CHARTS & SCORES

MAPS

ARCHITECTURAL
PLANS & DRAWINGS

INSTRUCTIONAL DIAGRAMS
FOR PRODUCTS

SCIENTIFIC
ILLUSTRATIONS

CITY OF NIAGARA (NEW YORK)
USA
AD:Robert Gersin
D:James Goldschmidt
I:Unk
DF:Robert P. Gersin Assoc. Inc.

**PENNSYLVANIA DEPARTMENT
OF TRANSPORTATION**
USA 1990
CD:Lois Morasco
AD,D:Joel Katz
I:Tom Jackson
DF:Katz Wheeler Design

Map showing major decision points in the City of Niagara Falls, NY.
ニューヨーク州ナイアガラ・フォール市の観光プランの分岐ポイントを示した地図。

Guide to Interstate-676 providing information about the new expressway.
新しい高速道路「州間道路676号線」の情報ガイド。

STATISTICAL
TABLES & GRAPHS

CHARTS & SCORES

MAPS

ARCHITECTURAL
PLANS & DRAWINGS

INSTRUCTIONAL DIAGRAMS
FOR PRODUCTS

SCIENTIFIC
ILLUSTRATIONS

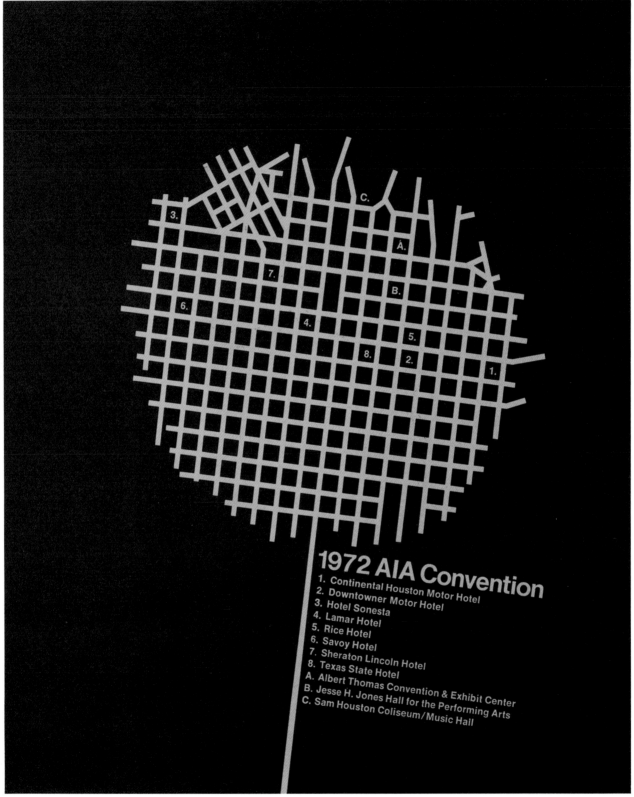

1972 AIA Convention
1. Continental Houston Motor Hotel
2. Downtowner Motor Hotel
3. Hotel Sonesta
4. Lamar Hotel
5. Rice Hotel
6. Savoy Hotel
7. Sheraton Lincoln Hotel
8. Texas State Hotel
A. Albert Thomas Convention & Exhibit Center
B. Jesse H. Jones Hall for the Performing Arts
C. Sam Houston Coliseum/Music Hall

Street map of Houston, Texas where an AIA (American Institute of Architects) national convention was held. From a poster.
AIA（アメリカ建築家協会）国際会議ポスターより、会議の会場となったテキサス州ヒューストン市の街路図。

THE NATIONAL GRID
ENGLAND 1990
CD,AD,D:John McConnell
D:Justus Oehler
DF:Pentagram Design Ltd.

STATISTICAL
TABLES & GRAPHS

CHARTS & SCORES

MAPS

ARCHITECTURAL
PLANS & DRAWINGS

INSTRUCTIONAL DIAGRAMS
FOR PRODUCTS

SCIENTIFIC
ILLUSTRATIONS

Map showing the locations of power stations. From a National Grid business report.
ナショナルグリッド社の業務報告書より、発電所の位置を示す地図。

STATISTICAL
TABLES & GRAPHS

CHARTS & SCORES

MAPS

ARCHITECTURAL
PLANS & DRAWINGS

INSTRUCTIONAL DIAGRAMS
FOR PRODUCTS

SCIENTIFIC
ILLUSTRATIONS

Location map of the commercial building Axis. From a promotional pamphlet.
プロモーション用パンフレットより、テナントビル「アクシス」の所在地図。

STATISTICAL
TABLES & GRAPHS

CHARTS & SCORES

MAPS

ARCHITECTURAL
PLANS & DRAWINGS

INSTRUCTIONAL DIAGRAMS
FOR PRODUCTS

SCIENTIFIC
ILLUSTRATIONS

AZABU BUILDING CO., LTD.
JAPAN 1989
AD:Ichiro Higashiizumi
D:Kazuhiro Kishi/Yumiko Iizuka
DF:Huia Media Design Co., Ltd.

ASAHI SHIMBUN AERA DIVISION
JAPAN 1991
AD:Nobuko Edatsune
D:Nobuo Morishita

Map showing the location of the Joule-A Building.
Pictographs are used to explain public transportation routes to and from the building.
JOULE-Aビルの所在地図。交通機関の説明にピクトグラムが利用されている。

Graph for the article,
"Allotted number of representative seats for each constituency" in Aera magazine.
週刊誌「アエラ」より、"選挙区別定数"に関する記事に使用されたグラフ・マップ。

STATISTICAL
TABLES & GRAPHS

CHARTS & SCORES

MAPS

ARCHITECTURAL
PLANS & DRAWINGS

INSTRUCTIONAL DIAGRAMS
FOR PRODUCTS

SCIENTIFIC
ILLUSTRATIONS

MARATHON REALTY COMPANY LIMITED,
BUILDINGS GROUP
CANADA 1991
AD,D:Roslyn Eskind
D,I:Peter Scott
DF:Eskind Waddell

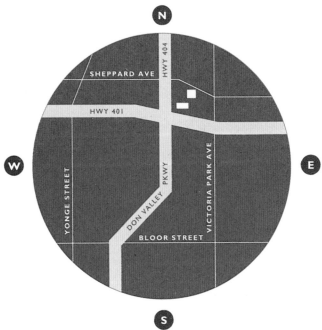

Site plan giving tenants of the commercial development a clear indication of building, parking and arterial road locations.
Map locating the development relative to major city access roads.
賃貸物件の便利性を示す、ビル・駐車場・幹線道路を含む商業開発区域平面図、及び都市につながる主要道路との位置関係地図。

TOKYO DOME KORAKUEN PARK 91-92

LOVE LOVE LOVE

1 ウルトラツイスター
2 スカイフラワー
3 スカイサイクル
4 フライングキャビンUFO
5 フライングカーペット
6 後楽園タワー
7 トラバント
8 お化け屋敷
9 バルーン
10 ギディスウィング
11 サーカストレイン
12 ティーカップ
13 小メリーゴーランド
14 ラブエクスプレス
15 レインボー
16 キディランド
17 野外劇場
18 スーパーシャトル
19 スーパーテレコンバット
20 豆汽車
21 ジェットコースター
22 バイキング
23 大メリーゴーランド
24 ミラーワールド
25 大観覧車
26 チビッコ広場
27 カーニバル

Guide map of Korakuen Amusement Park in Tokyo. Printed on the admission ticket.
チケットに印刷された東京後楽園遊園地の案内地図。

STATISTICAL
TABLES & GRAPHS

CHARTS & SCORES

MAPS

ARCHITECTURAL
PLANS & DRAWINGS

INSTRUCTIONAL DIAGRAMS
FOR PRODUCTS

SCIENTIFIC
ILLUSTRATIONS

STATISTICAL
TABLES & GRAPHS

CHARTS & SCORES

MAPS

ARCHITECTURAL
PLANS & DRAWINGS

INSTRUCTIONAL DIAGRAMS
FOR PRODUCTS

SCIENTIFIC
ILLUSTRATIONS

Location stand guide for Four Oaks horticultural exhibition.
フォアオークス園芸展示会場の所在地を示すスタンド案内図。

STATISTICAL
TABLES & GRAPHS

CHARTS & SCORES

MAPS

ARCHITECTURAL
PLANS & DRAWINGS

INSTRUCTIONAL DIAGRAMS
FOR PRODUCTS

SCIENTIFIC
ILLUSTRATIONS

CITY OF LONDON POLICE
ENGLAND 1992
AD: Tom Griffin
D: Ian Moore
DF: Griffin Associates

Snow Hill Police Station

Wood Street Police Building

Force Headquarters Old Jewry

Bishopsgate Police Station

- ● Underground Stations
- ◉ Bank link to Waterloo Station
- ■ British Rail

- - - - Divisional boundary
———— Force boundary

City of London Police Force Boundaries Map
ロンドン市警察の管轄区域図。

LAMBTON PLACE
ENGLAND 1987
CD:David Pearce
AD,D:Amanda Tatham
DF:Lambton Place

TATHAM · DAVID PEARCE · RICHARD WARD

AMANDA · LIZ JAMES · LORA STARLING

TELEPHONE · 01-221 2248

8 LAMBTON PLACE LONDON W11 2SH

Location map of the design firm Lambton Place.
デザイン事務所「ラムトン・プレース」の所在地図。

STATISTICAL TABLES & GRAPHS

CHARTS & SCORES

MAPS

ARCHITECTURAL PLANS & DRAWINGS

INSTRUCTIONAL DIAGRAMS FOR PRODUCTS

SCIENTIFIC ILLUSTRATIONS

STATISTICAL
TABLES & GRAPHS

CHARTS & SCORES

MAPS

ARCHITECTURAL
PLANS & DRAWINGS

INSTRUCTIONAL DIAGRAMS
FOR PRODUCTS

SCIENTIFIC
ILLUSTRATIONS

1. MCI
USA 1985
CD,AD,D:Susan Hochbaum
I:Steven Guarnaccia
DF:Pentagram Design Ltd.

2. SEAGRAM LONDON
ENGLAND 1990
CD,AD:Amanda Tatham
D:Paul Hannan
I:Michael Hill
DF:Tatham Pearce Ltd.

3. DEL MAR PLAZA
USA 1990
AD:Brenda Bodney
D,I:Tracy Sabin
DF:Bodney/Siedler Design

1. Stylized map of the world serviced by MCI, a telephone communications company. From an annual report.
電信電話会社MCIのアニュアルリポートより、同社によりサービスを受ける地域のイラストレーションマップ。

2. Seagram London's new building location map
ロンドン・シーグラム社の新ビル所在地図。

3. Del Mar Plaza location map used in brochures.
パンフレットに使用されたデルマルプラザ所在地図。

STATISTICAL
TABLES &
GRAPHS

CHARTS & SCORES

MAPS

ARCHITECTURAL
PLANS &
DRAWINGS

INSTRUCTIONAL
DIAGRAMS
FOR PRODUCTS

SCIENTIFIC
ILLUSTRATIONS

**THE FUND FOR
THE BOROUGH OF BROOKLYN, INC.**
USA 1984
CD,AD,D:Keith Godard
I:Cadre Graphics
DF:Studio Works

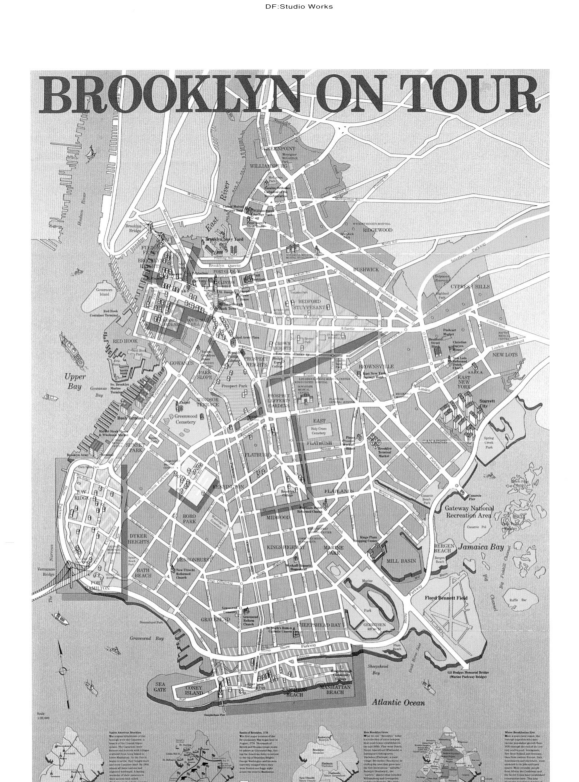

"Brooklyn On Tour" is an all-in-one map and guide to America's favorite hometown, Brooklyn.
「ブルックリン巡り」はアメリカで人気のホームタウン/ブルックリンの地図とガイドを一括で見ることができる。

APT·AZIENDA
PER LA PROMOZIONE TURISTICA
DELLA PROVINCIA DI FERRARA
ITALY 1989,1990
AD:Craziano Uillani
D,I:Cinzia Calzolari

53RD STREET ASSOC.
USA
AD:Collin Forbes
D:Kaspar Schmid/Michael Gericke
I:Steven Guarnaccia

STATISTICAL TABLES & GRAPHS

CHARTS & SCORES

MAPS

ARCHITECTURAL PLANS & DRAWINGS

INSTRUCTIONAL DIAGRAMS FOR PRODUCTS

SCIENTIFIC ILLUSTRATIONS

Tourist itinerary map for promotion of Ferrara city.
フェラーラ市のプロモーション用に制作された観光ルート地図。

Map showing important cultural institutions on 53rd Street, including the Museum of Modern Art, NY.
ニューヨーク近代美術館を含む重要な文化施設を表した53番街の地図。

STATISTICAL
TABLES & GRAPHS

CHARTS & SCORES

MAPS

ARCHITECTURAL
PLANS & DRAWINGS

INSTRUCTIONAL DIAGRAMS
FOR PRODUCTS

SCIENTIFIC
ILLUSTRATIONS

YAMANASHI PREFECTURE

JAPAN 1988

AD:Tokihiro Okuda

D:Mitsuko Kato

I:Fumiyo Kojima

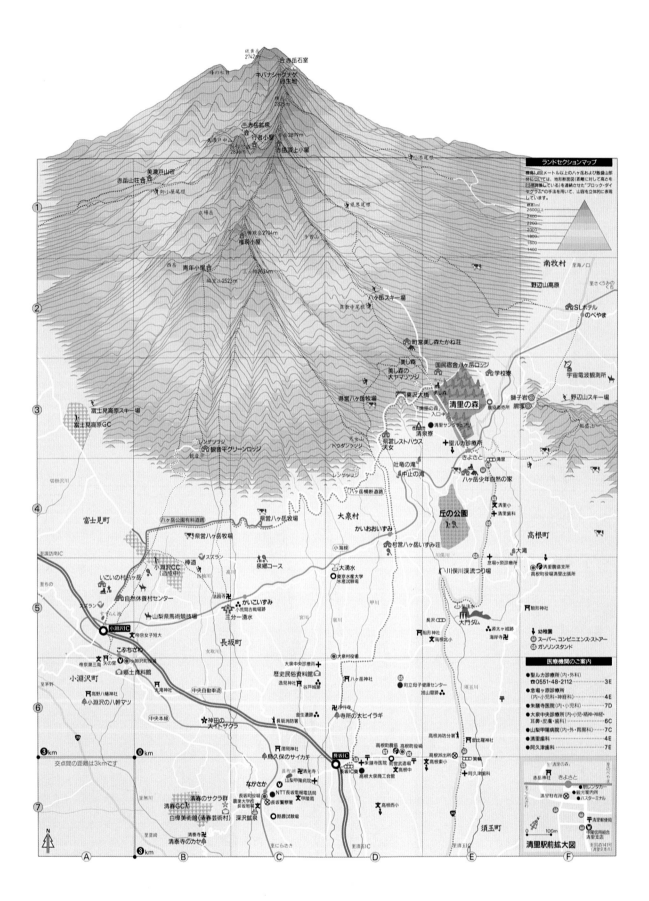

Map used in a leaflet advertising real estate in the Kiyosatonomori resort area.

別荘用分譲地のパンフレットより、リゾート地「清里の森」の地図。

STATISTICAL
TABLES &
GRAPHS

CHARTS & SCORES

MAPS

ARCHITECTURAL
PLANS & DRAWINGS

INSTRUCTIONAL DIAGRAMS
FOR PRODUCTS

SCIENTIFIC
ILLUSTRATIONS

NATIONAL GEOGRAPHIC MAGAZINE
USA 1991
CD:Allen Carroll
AD:John F. Dorr
D:Sally S. Summerall
I:John Dawson
DF:Carto Graphic Division of
National Geog. Magazine

"Africa Threatened" map carried in the appendix of National Geographic Magazine reporting in detail on the current situation of various endangered species throughout Africa.
「ナショナル・ジオグラフィック・マガジン」の付録に使用された"アフリカへの脅威"地図。アフリカ各地で絶滅の危機に瀕している動物たちの現況を詳しく報告している。

STATISTICAL
TABLES & GRAPHS

CHARTS & SCORES

MAPS

ARCHITECTURAL
PLANS & DRAWINGS

INSTRUCTIONAL DIAGRAMS
FOR PRODUCTS

SCIENTIFIC
ILLUSTRATIONS

CLUB MED, INC.
USA 1991
CD,D,I:Stephen Ferrari
DF:The Graphic Expression, Inc.

**3,400
North American
GMs visited the
European zone**

**5,400
North American
GMs visited the
Asian zone**

**55,900
European and
South American
GMs visited the
American zone**

Map showing regional travel among Club Med Asian and American zones.
会員制クラブ「クラブ・メッド」のアジア・アメリカ旅行における地域施設案内図。

STATISTICAL
TABLES & GRAPHS

CHARTS & SCORES

MAPS

ARCHITECTURAL
PLANS & DRAWINGS

INSTRUCTIONAL
DIAGRAMS
FOR PRODUCTS

SCIENTIFIC
ILLUSTRATIONS

WINDSTAR CRUISES
USA 1991
AD,D:Jack Anderson
D:Denise Weir/Paula Cox
I:Bruce Morser
DF:Hornall Anderson Design Works

21,000
European zone
GMs visited
the Asian zone

2,200
Asian GMs
visited the
European zone

2,400
Asian GMs
visited the
American zone

Maps showing the ports of call of Windstar Cruises. From a Windstar Cruises brochure.
ウィンドスター・クルージィーズ社のカタログより、クルーズ・ツアーの寄航地を示す地図。

STATISTICAL
TABLES & GRAPHS

CHARTS & SCORES

MAPS

ARCHITECTURAL
PLANS & DRAWINGS

INSTRUCTIONAL DIAGRAMS
FOR PRODUCTS

SCIENTIFIC
ILLUSTRATIONS

NORCEN ENERGY RESOURCES
USA 1990,1991
AD:Kit Hinrichs
D:Piper Murakami
I:Max Seabaugh
DF:Pentagram Design Ltd.

STATISTICAL
TABLES & GRAPHS

CHARTS & SCORES

MAPS

ARCHITECTURAL
PLANS & DRAWINGS

INSTRUCTIONAL DIAGRAMS
FOR PRODUCTS

SCIENTIFIC
ILLUSTRATIONS

Maps showing areas developed and operated by Norcen Energy Resources. From an annual report.
ノーセン・エナジー・リゾース社のアニュアルリポートより、開発地域や業務地域を表した地図。

STATISTICAL
TABLES & GRAPHS

CHARTS & SCORES

MAPS

ARCHITECTURAL
PLANS & DRAWINGS

INSTRUCTIONAL DIAGRAMS
FOR PRODUCTS

SCIENTIFIC
ILLUSTRATIONS

ARCO

USA 1988

CD:Ron Jefferies

D,I:Ken Lotz

DF:The Jefferies Association

NORTH SLOPE OF ALASKA

ARCO has been a major participant in oil and gas exploration and development in Alaska since 1957, when the Company discovered the Swanson River field, the state's first commercial oil field, on the Kenai Peninsula.

In 1969, ARCO discovered the Kuparuk River field in a joint venture with British Petroleum.

ARCO is operator of three fields currently producing on the North Slope and has an interest in several other areas.

In 1968, as operator for itself and Exxon, ARCO discovered the Prudhoe Bay field, the largest oil field ever found in the United States.

PRUDHOE BAY

Working interest:
Crude oil — 21.78%
Natural gas and condensate — 42.56%
NGLs — 33% (1987 average)

Original oil in place:
22 billion barrels (gross)

Remaining net reserves at 12-31-87: 1,442 MMB

Started production: 1977

1987 liquids production (MB/D):
Crude oil — 1,504 gross/280 net
Condensate — 64 gross/23 net
NGLs — 40 gross/12 net

1987 development wells drilled:
34 gross/8 net

Producing wells at year end:
675 gross/147 net

KUPARUK

Working interest: 56.3%

Original oil in place:
5 billion barrels (gross)

Remaining net reserves at 12-31-87: 604 MMB

Started production: 1981

1987 liquids production (MB/D):
283 gross/124 net

1987 development wells drilled:
45 gross/25 net

Producing wells at year end:
329 gross/185 net

LISBURNE

Working interest: 40%

Original oil in place:
1.3 billion barrels (gross)

Remaining net reserves at 12-31-87: 70 MMB

Started production: 1986

1987 liquids production (MB/D):
45 gross/15 net

1987 development wells drilled:
18 gross/7 net

Producing wells at year end:
47 gross/19 net

WEST SAK

Working interest:
Undetermined

Original oil in place:
10-20 billion barrels (gross)

1987 activity:
3 delineation wells drilled as "post holes"

Expected start up:
mid to late 1990s

ANWR COASTAL PLAIN

1987 activity:
Acquired a potential interest in acreage through agreements with two Alaskan native groups. Farmed out interest in Aurora well to gain subsurface information.

Legend
■ ARCO Full Interest Acreage
■ ARCO Partial Interest Acreage
■ Potential ARCO Full Interest Acreage
(Subject to approval of native land exchange agreements)
○ Well (currently drilling or recently drilled)

GULF OF MEXICO

The offshore Gulf of Mexico is a prime gas producing area for ARCO and also an area of present and future exploratory interest. ARCO currently has an interest in 156 developed blocks and 45 producing platforms in the Gulf. ARCO is operator of 44 of these platforms.

In the deep-water portion of the Gulf of Mexico, ARCO has an interest in 48 blocks.

42 of which are 100-percent ARCO owned. These blocks include 9 in Alaminos Canyon, 1 in Garden Banks, 7 in Green Canyon and 31 in Mississippi Canyon. Capital expenditures associated with deep-water Gulf activities totaled $29 million in 1987.

MAJOR FIELDS IN WHICH ARCO HAS AN INTEREST
( ) represents working interest

South Pass Block 61
(100%)
Started production 1971
1987 net production
oil — 16,200 B/D
gas (sales) — 1.8 MMCF/D

Matagorda Island 668
(85%)
Started production 1985
1987 net gas sales 96.1 MMCF/D

West Cameron 205
(100%)
Started production 1982
1987 net production
oil — 1,700 B/D
gas (sales) — 64.4 MMCF/D

West Cameron Block 66
(33.50%)
Started production 1976
1987 net production
oil — 1,500 B/D
gas (sales) — 14.1 MMCF/D

Matagorda Island 703
(100%)
Started production 1983
1987 net gas sales
19.9 MMCF/D

High Island 116
(100%)
Started production 1986
1987 net production
873 MMCF/D

Grand Isle Block 43
(25%)
Started production 1956
1987 net production
oil — 3,400 B/D
gas (sales) — 15 MMCF/D

High Island Block A-467
(100%)
Started production 1982
1987 net gas sales
44.7 MMCF/D

Ship Shoal 332
(100%)
Started production 1986
1987 net production
oil — 1,600 B/D
gas (sales) — 33.4 MMCF/D

High Island A-20
(100%)
Started production 1985
1987 net gas sales
41.7 MMCF/D

Grand Isle Block 47
(25%)
Started production 1955
1987 net production
oil — 1,900 B/D
gas (sales) — 9.2 MMCF/D

West Cameron Block 237
(100%)
Started production 1979
1987 net gas sales
34.9 MMCF/D

Mississippi Canyon Block 148
(48%)
Started production 1981
1987 net gas sales
29.6 MMCF/D

Main Pass Block 129
(100%)
Expected start up 1988

Legend
■ ARCO Full Interest Acreage
■ ARCO Partial Interest Acreage
■ Oil Field
 Gas Field
 ARCO operated Platform(s)

Simple line art maps showing very complicated exploration and production locations.
非常に複雑な実地探究や生産の立地を単純な線で示すアートマップ。

STATISTICAL
TABLES & GRAPHS

CHARTS & SCORES

MAPS

ARCHITECTURAL
PLANS & DRAWINGS

INSTRUCTIONAL DIAGRAMS
FOR PRODUCTS

SCIENTIFIC
ILLUSTRATIONS

ARCO
USA 1991
CD:Ron Jefferies
D:Scott Lambert
P:Keith Wood
I:Hank Fisher
DF:The Jefferies Association

"We continue to see a promising future in Indonesia where we have been active for nearly 25 years. We have already discovered more than 1 billion barrels of oil and condensate in the Java Sea and are still bringing on stream discoveries, like the BZZ field that was discovered in 1988. Our large Pagerungan gas field, in the Kangean block offshore Bali, is moving toward production."

A 3-D seismic survey of the BZZ field offshore in ARCO's contract area of the Northwest Java Sea of Indonesia allowed detailed mapping of the reservoir from which production will begin in 1991. Hydrocarbons in this field are trapped within carbonate and clastic reservoirs of Oligocene to Eocene ages.

This diagram shows an anticline bounded by a major fault and syncline.

The main accumulation of hydrocarbon reserves is trapped in the separate closure, within the anticline, seen in the center of the diagram.

"We have continued to see demand growth for gasoline in our five-state marketing area, but economic conditions and improved public transportation could moderate this growth. Our formula is to maintain low price leadership while increasing marketing opportunities with am/pm mini markets and our new SMOGPROS service centers which have proved to be highly popular."

Washington has 209 branded outlets of which 100 are am/pm mini markets. Oregon has 89 outlets of which 29 are am/pm sites.

In Nevada, 50 of 76 branded outlets are am/pm sites, while in Arizona, ARCO has 75 outlets of which 83 are am/pm locations.

California has 1,098 branded outlets of which 510 are am/pm's and 112 are SMOGPROS. Six of the California am/pm's are mini markets only with no gasoline sales.

■ Refinery

● Distribution Terminal

26

14

ARCO is a participant in offshore drilling programs that are continuing in the Chukchi Sea, 350 miles from the State's large North Slope oil fields.

Prudhoe Bay and Kuparuk are situated on Alaska's North Slope. Lisburne underlies Prudhoe Bay and is adjacent to Point McIntyre. Additional development continues in these areas.

Exploration projects are active offshore in the Beaufort Sea where ARCO drilled two prospects in 1990 and plans more in 1991.

ARCO drilled one prospect in Cook Inlet in 1990 and expects to return for additional drilling during 1991.

H.L. "Skip" Bilhartz
President
ARCO Alaska, Inc.

"Alaska is considered to hold significant potential for more large oil discoveries, and ARCO wants to be part of those. We are pursuing a balanced and well reasoned exploration program. We have already improved our competitive position using our exploration information, and we will be seeking new leases as they become available."

■ ARCO exploration drilling 1990-1991

▲ Exploration drilling/ ARCO participation 1990-1991

● ARCO operational facilities

ARCO Coal Australia has interests in four mines in the State of Queensland (from left to right) Blair Athol, Gordonstone, Curragh, and Coal Resources of Queensland (CRQ). The mines are all located in the Bowen Basin within 100 miles of one another.

Coal from ARCO's Australian mines moves through the ports of Gladstone and Mackay to Asia and as far as Europe and South America. ARCO Coal Australia's headquarters are in Brisbane.

Anthony G. Fernandes
President
ARCO Coal Co.

"ARCO Coal has been producing coal in Australia for just seven years and already ARCO Coal Australia is one of the country's largest coal companies. Our investments are increasing. The development of Gordonstone will give us the largest underground coal mine in the country, with production expected to begin in 1992. Capacity expansion is also in process at Curragh."

■ Seaport

● Coal Mine

▲ Headquarters

29

Maps designed to look like color-enhanced space photos, created on a Macintosh computer. From an Arco annual report.
アルコ社のアニュアルリポートより、色彩を強調し、宇宙写真をイメージしてマッキントッシュ・コンピューターでデザインされた地図。

STATISTICAL
TABLES & GRAPHS

CHARTS & SCORES

MAPS

ARCHITECTURAL
PLANS & DRAWINGS

INSTRUCTIONAL DIAGRAMS
FOR PRODUCTS

SCIENTIFIC
ILLUSTRATIONS

UNOCAL CORPORATION
USA 1987,1988,1990,1991
CD,AD,D,I:Ray Engle
I:Debra Hampton
DF:Ray Engle & Associates

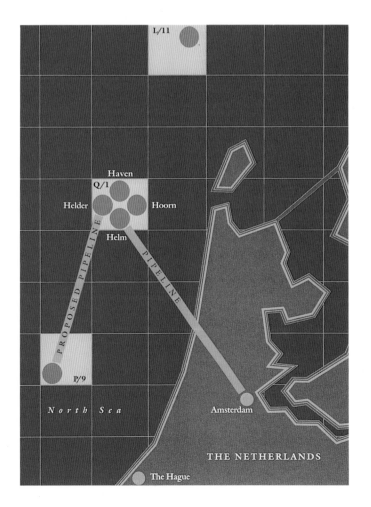

STATISTICAL
TABLES & GRAPHS

CHARTS & SCORES

MAPS

ARCHITECTURAL
PLANS & DRAWINGS

INSTRUCTIONAL DIAGRAMS
FOR PRODUCTS

SCIENTIFIC
ILLUSTRATIONS

● ONSHORE FIELDS
◉ OFFSHORE PRODUCING FIELDS
□ OFFSHORE LEASED AREAS

● REFINERIES
■ CRUDE PIPELINES
■ PRODUCT PIPELINES

Maps showing the development and production of petroleum resources in various parts of the world. From a magazine article.
雑誌記事より、世界各地における石油資源の開発、及び生産に関する地図。

GARBAGE MAGAZINE
USA 1991
AD,D:Rob George
D,I:Scott A. MacNeill

PHIBRO ENERGY, INC.
USA 1992
AD:Howard Belk
D:Dana Gonsalvez
I:In House
DF:Belk Mignogna Associates Ltd.

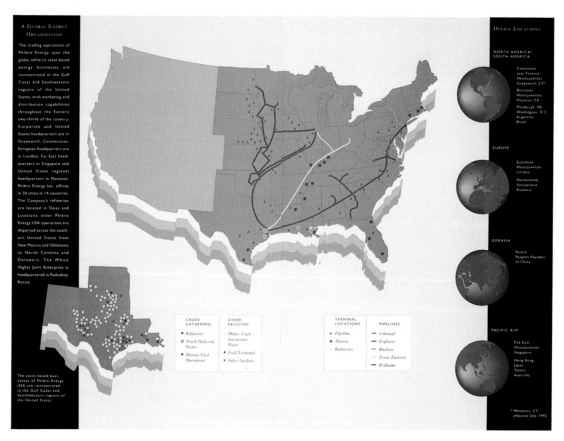

ARCHITECTURAL
PLANS & DRAWINGS

INSTRUCTIONAL DIAGRAMS
FOR PRODUCTS

SCIENTIFIC
ILLUSTRATIONS

Map locating the top polluters in the USA
by state and business with each state's pollution per person level.
アメリカの州や産業別でトップに位置する汚染源のデータを表した地図。

Map illustrating Phibro's marketing and distribution capabilities.
The smaller map illustrates the asset-based energy businesses concentrated in the Gulf Coast Region.
The globes show Phibro's office locations. From a Phibro Energy Inc. annual report.
ファイブロ社のアニュアルリポートより、同社のマーケティング能力や流通能力を表す地図、及び事務所の所在地を表す地球図。

U.S.NEWS & WORLD REPORT
USA 1992
D,I:Matt Zang

TIME MAGAZINE
USA 1992
AD:Nigel Holmes
D:Joe Lertola/Paul Pugliese/Steve Hart

Map showing nuclear-related facilities in the former Soviet Union. From U.S. News & World Report magazine.
「USニュース & ワールド・リポートマガジン」より、旧ソ連邦における核関連施設を示す地図。

Albertville Olympics map from Time magazine.
「タイムマガジン」より、アルベールビル・オリンピックの会場地図。

STATISTICAL
TABLES & GRAPHS

CHARTS & SCORES

MAPS

ARCHITECTURAL
PLANS & DRAWINGS

INSTRUCTIONAL DIAGRAMS
FOR PRODUCTS

SCIENTIFIC
ILLUSTRATIONS

Map showing the positions of all the troops, air bases, oil fields, pipelines and ships involved in the 1991 Gulf War. From Time magazine.
「タイムマガジン」より、1991年の湾岸戦争に関連した軍隊、空軍基地、油田、パイプラインなどの位置を網羅した地図。

1. INHOUSE
ENGLAND 1991
CD,AD,D,I:Richard Schedler
P:Dave Denham

2. BRITISH TRUST FOR
YOUNG ACHIEVERS
ENGLAND 1991
CD,AD,D,I:Richard Schedler/
Marcus Kelly
P:Dave Denham

3. ALLIED INSURANCE BROKERS
ENGLAND 1992
CD,AD:Philip Kruger
D,I:Richard Schedler
P:Dave Denham

STATISTICAL
TABLES & GRAPHS

CHARTS & SCORES

MAPS

ARCHITECTURAL
PLANS & DRAWINGS

INSTRUCTIONAL DIAGRAMS
FOR PRODUCTS

SCIENTIFIC
ILLUSTRATIONS

4. 6. BBC TELEVISION, NEWS
AND CURRENT AFFAIRS
ENGLAND 1991,1992
D:Kaye Huddy/Jean Cramond
DF:N/CA Graphic Design Department
BBC Television

5. EUROPCAR
ENGLAND 1992
CD,AD,D,I:Marcus Kelly
(The Presentation Co. Brussels)
P:Jerome Zimmerman

Visualized maps produced for corporate or TV presentation.
テレビ番組や企業のプレゼンテーションの映像用に制作されたマップ。

STATISTICAL
TABLES & GRAPHS

CHARTS & SCORES

MAPS

ARCHITECTURAL
PLANS & DRAWINGS

INSTRUCTIONAL DIAGRAMS
FOR PRODUCTS

SCIENTIFIC
ILLUSTRATIONS

BRITISH STEEL PLC
ENGLAND 1992
CD:Geoff Aldridge
AD,I:Sally Mcintosh
D:Joseph Mitchell
I:Barry Brocklebank
DF:Communication by Design

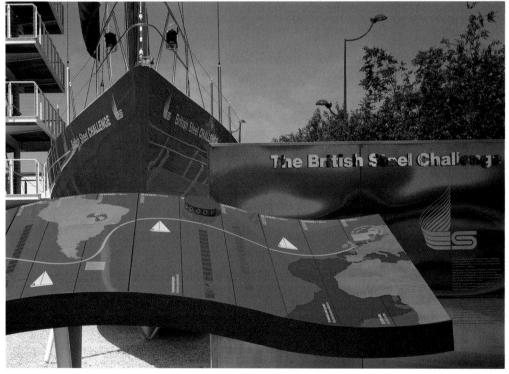

Giant route map of the round-the world yacht race "British Steel Challenge". Displayed at the British Pavilion in Expo'92.
Expo'92 の英国パビリオンに展示された、世界一周ヨットレース「ブリティッシュ・スティール・チャレンジ」の巨大なルートマップ。

STATISTICAL
TABLES & GRAPHS

CHARTS & SCORES

MAPS

ARCHITECTURAL
PLANS & DRAWINGS

INSTRUCTIONAL DIAGRAMS
FOR PRODUCTS

SCIENTIFIC
ILLUSTRATIONS

ADVERTISING WOMEN OF NEW YORK
USA 1989
CD,AD,D,I:Keith Godard
D:Jamie Jett Walker
P:John T. Hill
DF:Studio Works

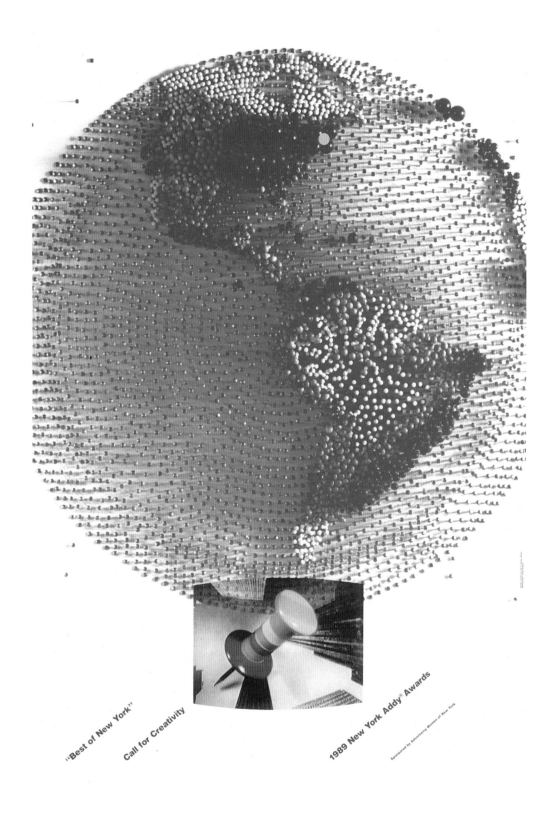

Global map is made up of pins representing the population of the western hemisphere.
The large dark pins represent over population and the small white pins represent no population.
ピンによる西半球人口地図。大きく濃い色のピンは人口過剰地帯、小さい白色のピンは無人口地帯を表している。

STATISTICAL
TABLES & GRAPHS

CHARTS & SCORES

MAPS

ARCHITECTURAL
PLANS & DRAWINGS

INSTRUCTIONAL DIAGRAMS
FOR PRODUCTS

SCIENTIFIC
ILLUSTRATIONS

JOHN PORTMAN COMPANIES
USA 1991
AD:Lowell Williams
D:Bill Carson
I:Andy Dearwater
DF:Pentagram Design Ltd.

Bounded by Peachtree Street, Peachtree Center Avenue, and Baker Street, One Peachtree Center's location in downtown Atlanta is ideal, close to the greatest concentration of amenities, with unparalleled access to the rest of the city.

Location map of a high-rise building, One Peachtree Center, in Atlanta. From a promotional pamphlet.
プロモーション用パンフレットより、アトランタの高層ビル「ワンピーチツリー・センター」の所在地図。

TurnerCity 1989

A representation of buildings Turner completed around the world in 1989

The Key to the City

STATISTICAL
TABLES & GRAPHS

CHARTS & SCORES

MAPS

ARCHITECTURAL
PLANS & DRAWINGS

INSTRUCTIONAL DIAGRAMS
FOR PRODUCTS

SCIENTIFIC
ILLUSTRATIONS

REUTERS LIMITED
ENGLAND 1984
AD,D:Mervyn Kurlansky
D:Robert Maude
I:Roger Taylor/Richard Clifton-Dey
DF:Pentagram Design Ltd.

Communications map showing points of contact across the globe.
地球に張りめぐらされた通信ポイントを示す通信網の地図。

STATISTICAL
TABLES & GRAPHS

CHARTS & SCORES

MAPS

ARCHITECTURAL
PLANS & DRAWINGS

INSTRUCTIONAL DIAGRAMS
FOR PRODUCTS

SCIENTIFIC
ILLUSTRATIONS

SERVICES GROUP OF AMERICA
USA
AD,D:Jack Anderson
D:Mike Courtney
DF:Hornall Anderson Design Works

Wall map showing the member companies of Services Group of America.
サービスグループ・オブ・アメリカ社の会社所在地を示すウォール・マップ。

STATISTICAL
TABLES & GRAPHS

CHARTS & SCORES

MAPS

ARCHITECTURAL
PLANS & DRAWINGS

INSTRUCTIONAL DIAGRAMS
FOR PRODUCTS

SCIENTIFIC
ILLUSTRATIONS

Connectivity map of a global telecommunications network. The map's graphic shape, two intersecting circles, recalls MasterCard International's corporate trade mark.
世界規模の電子通信ネットワークを表した地図。この地図の2つの円が重なり合っている形はマスターカード・インターナショナル社のブランドマークを象徴している。

STATISTICAL
TABLES & GRAPHS

CHARTS & SCORES

MAPS

ARCHITECTURAL
PLANS & DRAWINGS

INSTRUCTIONAL DIAGRAMS
FOR PRODUCTS

SCIENTIFIC
ILLUSTRATIONS

**THE SEIBU GROUP OF
RETAIL ENTERPRISES**
JAPAN 1981
CD,AD,D:Tetsuya Ohta

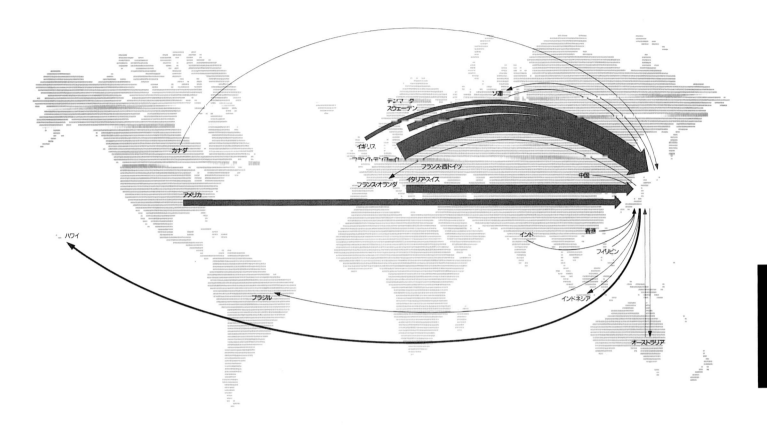

Map of the global penetration (export, import) of the Seibu Group of Retail Enterprises.
西武流通グループの世界展開（輸出量・輸入量）を解説する地図。

STATISTICAL
TABLES & GRAPHS

CHARTS & SCORES

MAPS

ARCHITECTURAL
PLANS & DRAWINGS

INSTRUCTIONAL DIAGRAMS
FOR PRODUCTS

SCIENTIFIC
ILLUSTRATIONS

The dimaxion map invented by Buckminster Fuller; the most accurate way to show the size of areas and distances.
バックミンスター・フラーが考案した、面積や距離が最も正確に表されている世界地図「ダイマクシオンマップ」。

建築プラン

マップが区域や地域という、移動を前提とする大きな空間を描くことを基本としていたのに対して、ここに紹介する建築プランは、むしろ居住や販売、展示を目的とした、中規模以下の人造の空間を描いたものである。無論、建築プランのなかには、公園さらには都市といった大規模な空間を描くものも多いのだが、それらとマップの本質的な違いは、地図があくまで既存の空間の「案内」や「解説」を目的としているのに対して、プランは常に、その立案、設計といったクリエイティブな関心を背景に、検討、吟味、ないしはプレゼンテーションのために描かれている点にある。

いうまでもないことながら、ダイアグラムは二次元の表現である。マップという空間を描くダイアグラムもさることながら、プランには、二次元の画面に三次元の空間を描くことの興味があふれている。このことは、マップに関してもいえるのだが、マップが空間を広がりとして、むしろ二次元的に描く傾向が強いのに対して、プランには、立体的な箱状の空間を二次元にいかに再現してみせるかという造形的課題がある分だけ、空間の表現に関してはスリリングな視覚的な工夫に富んでいる。

もともと、ルネッサンス以降の西洋絵画の最大の関心も、三次元空間をいかに二次元の画面にだまし絵的に再現し得るかという、透視図法による遠近法の完成にあった。レオナルド・ダ・ヴィンチの名高い『最後の晩餐』や、ラファエロの『アテナイの学園』など、ルネッサンス絵画の最高峰の作品が、同時にきわめてすぐれた建築図であるのはそのためである。

したがって、建築プランには、そういった絵画的表現の魅惑のもっとも基本的な要素が含まれている。具体的には、立体感を表わすための影の表現の工夫、建築物の内部を屋根や壁を通して描く透視図法の工夫などが、デザイン上の見せ場になるが、あたかもそこに三次元空間があるかのような錯覚を起こさせる絵画的な美しさや完成度と同時に、どこにどのような空間があり、それらがどのような構造でつながっているのかという、空間の「仕組み」や「仕掛け」の明快な表示するという、ダイアグラム本来の視覚的な機能性というものを重視する必要がある。

ARCHITECTURAL
PLANS & DRAWINGS

ARCHITECTURAL PLANS & DRAWINGS

Architectural plans are qualitatively and quantitatively different from maps. A map generally depicts a very large area, such as a territory or region, through which travel is implied. Architectural plans illustrate man-made structures which are on a smaller scale and which are intended as space for living, working or exhibiting things. Architectural plans do exist, of course, which deal with larger spaces such as parks and cities, but an essential difference remains; a map is always intended as a guide to and explanation of an already existing place. Architectural plans are always created as material either for the presentation of a project idea or as a guide to the actual construction of a project.

It goes without saying that a diagram is a two-dimensional image, and in the case of a map, the space described is, in essence, a two-dimensional plane. For the most part, it is simply a matter of scaling down the outlines of what is already there. Architectural plans, on the other hand, call for more interesting graphic solutions because they have to illustrate 3-D space on the 2-D surface. For the designer, this presents a number of challenges and options. Architectural plans will tend to demonstrate more clever visual contrivances where the expression of space is concerned, because that space must contain volume.

One of the main concerns in Western art after the Renaissance was how the artist could produce a 3-D effect on the surface of his canvas. This lead to the perfection of perspective drawings which employed a visual trick called the vanishing point. It is not surprising that masterpieces of Renaissance art such as "The Last Supper" by Leonardo Da Vinci and "School of Athens" by Raphael, in addition to being great paintings, are also superb examples of architectural drawing.

In architectural drawings, some of the basic elements of painterly technique are employed. Shadow is used, for example, to create a sense of depth and so forth, as well as illustrator's tricks such as cutaways to show the interior of a building through its roof or walls. Architectural plans, in other words, can serve as a showplace for design and illustration skills. Ultimately, however, aside from artistic beauty and illustrative tricks to create the illusion of 3-D space, the designer cannot lose sight of the original function of his drawing, which is that of a diagram. In architectural drawings, it is the structure and organization of space that we are interested in.

建築 プ ラ ン

STATISTICAL
TABLES & GRAPHS

CHARTS & SCORES

MAPS

ARCHITECTURAL
PLANS & DRAWINGS

INSTRUCTIONAL DIAGRAMS
FOR PRODUCTS

SCIENTIFIC
ILLUSTRATIONS

MELVIN SIMON & ASSOCIATES
USA 1985
CD:Jon Jerde
D,I,DF:JPI

Two-dimensional isometric drawing for Circle Center, Indianapolis project, produced for a presentation.
プレゼンテーションのために制作されたインディアナポリス・サークルセンター計画のアイソメトリック。

STATISTICAL
TABLES & GRAPHS

CHARTS & SCORES

MAPS

ARCHITECTURAL
PLANS & DRAWINGS

INSTRUCTIONAL DIAGRAMS
FOR PRODUCTS

SCIENTIFIC
ILLUSTRATIONS

METERS 0 5 10
FEET 0 10 20 32

11

CUT AXONOMETRIC THROUGH SEQUENCE OF SPACES FROM MOSQUE TO FOUNTAIN.

Axonometric projection of a fountain for a mosque in Isfaham, Iran.
イラン・イスファハムのモスクに建設される噴水のアクソノメトリック。

STATISTICAL
TABLES & GRAPHS

CHARTS & SCORES

MAPS

ARCHITECTURAL
PLANS & DRAWINGS

INSTRUCTIONAL DIAGRAMS
FOR PRODUCTS

SCIENTIFIC
ILLUSTRATIONS

Diagram depicting 4-Torri Building in Takamatsu from 9 angles. From "Emerging Japanese Architects of the 1990's Exhibition".

「1990年代を代表する日本の新進建築家展」より、高松市4-Torriビルを9方向から描いたダイアグラム。

STATISTICAL
TABLES & GRAPHS

CHARTS & SCORES

MAPS

ARCHITECTURAL
PLANS & DRAWINGS

INSTRUCTIONAL DIAGRAMS
FOR PRODUCTS

SCIENTIFIC
ILLUSTRATIONS

BARCELONA TOWER   EIFFEL TOWER   TOKYO TOWER   HONGKONG BANK   BANK OF

ARCHITECTURAL
PLANS & DRAWINGS

INSTRUCTIONAL DIAGRAMS
FOR PRODUCTS

SCIENTIFIC
ILLUSTRATIONS

DAIBA

GINZA   ROCKERFELLER CENTRE   ARC HILLS   YOYOGI STADIUM

CHRYSLER BUILIDNG   STANDARD OIL   HANCOCK TOWER   EMPIRE STATE   WORLD TRADE   SEARS TOWER   600 TOWER

Illustration of the Millennium Tower project. An 800 meter-tall building with both intelligent office facilities and residential civic facilities.
インテリジェント・オフィス施設と住宅・都市施設を併せもつ全長800メートルの建造物ミレニアム・タワー計画の図解。

AT & T
USA
AD:Louis Nelson
D:Chris Micelli/Dawn O'Keef
DF:Louis Nelson Associates Inc.

STATISTICAL
TABLES & GRAPHS

CHARTS & SCORES

MAPS

ARCHITECTURAL
PLANS & DRAWINGS

INSTRUCTIONAL DIAGRAMS
FOR PRODUCTS

SCIENTIFIC
ILLUSTRATIONS

Dimensional diagrams illustrating the master plan for the AT & T, NY Communications Museum.
The diagrams show over 30,000 sq.ft. encompassing four levels, including all gallery spaces and adjacent areas.
3万平方メートル以上に及ぶ美術館/AT & Tニューヨーク・コミュニケーションズミュージアムの全ギャラリー空間、及び隣接区域を含むマスタープラン立体図解。

STATISTICAL
TABLES & GRAPHS

CHARTS & SCORES

MAPS

ARCHITECTURAL
PLANS & DRAWINGS

INSTRUCTIONAL DIAGRAMS
FOR PRODUCTS

SCIENTIFIC
ILLUSTRATIONS

THE CHAMBERS OF MICHAEL BECKMAN
ENGLAND 1992
D,DF:Eco-iD Evolution

Isometric composition of Eco-iD "Evolution" freestanding structure and complete office which can be extended and reduced as required.
必要に応じて伸縮自在な家具システム「Eco-iDエボリューション」をとりいれた、事務所のアイソメトリック構成図。

YUHUIN ART MUSEUM
JAPAN 1991
AD:Tatsuaki Yasuno
D:Susumu Utagawa
DF:T.Y.D. Inc.

STATISTICAL
TABLES & GRAPHS

CHARTS & SCORES

MAPS

ARCHITECTURAL
PLANS & DRAWINGS

INSTRUCTIONAL DIAGRAMS
FOR PRODUCTS

SCIENTIFIC
ILLUSTRATIONS

STATISTICAL
TABLES & GRAPHS

CHARTS & SCORES

MAPS

ARCHITECTURAL
PLANS & DRAWINGS

INSTRUCTIONAL DIAGRAMS
FOR PRODUCTS

SCIENTIFIC
ILLUSTRATIONS

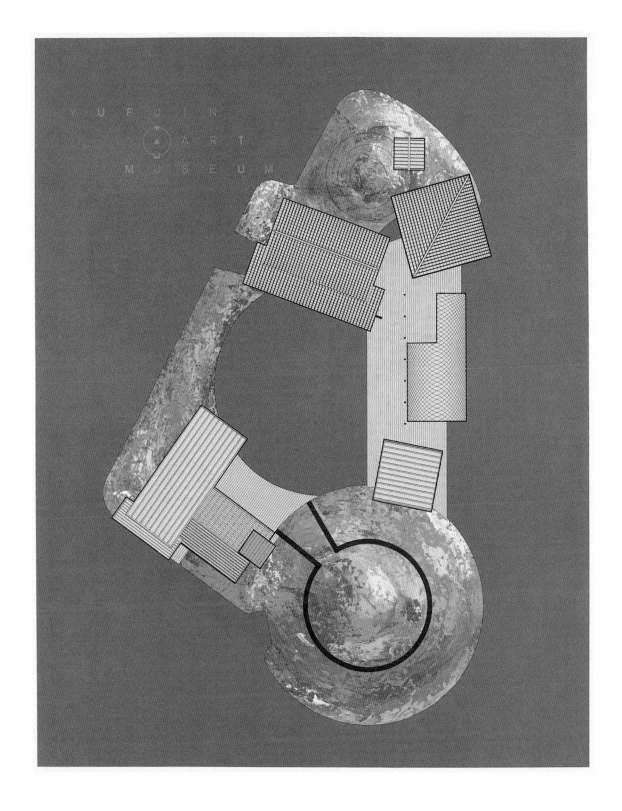

Architectural drawing for the Yuhuin Museum of Art in Oita Prefecture.

大分県「由布院美術館」の建築見取り図。

STATISTICAL
TABLES & GRAPHS

CHARTS & SCORES

MAPS

ARCHITECTURAL
PLANS & DRAWINGS

INSTRUCTIONAL DIAGRAMS
FOR PRODUCTS

SCIENTIFIC
ILLUSTRATIONS

SOLOMON R. GUGGENHEIM MUSEUM
AUSTRALIA 1991
CD:Pamela L. Myers
AD,D,I:Colin Rowan
DF:Powerhouse Museum Graphic Services &
The N.S.W Ministry for The Arts

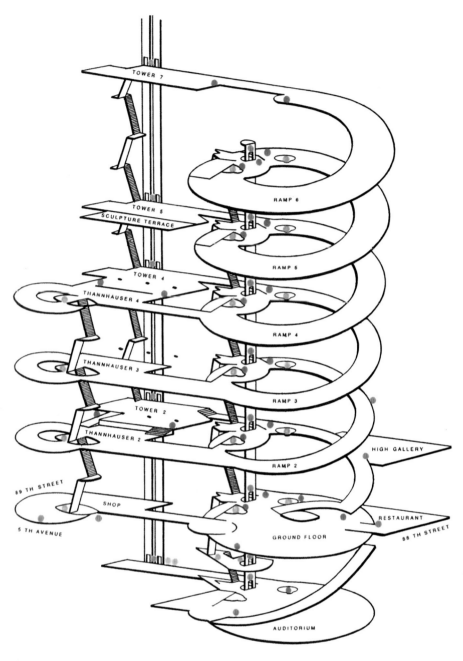

ガスメイ・シーゲル建築会社が制作したソロモン・R・グッゲンハイム美術館の設計図。

PERMANENT DIRECTIONAL SIGNAGE — For example: < Tower 4.

Probably wall mounted, directing visitors to building volumes and floor/ramp levels that are most frequently used as introductory galleries for the start of an exhibition or for overall circulation.

BUILDING VOLUME AND FLOOR / RAMP IDENTIFICATION — For example: Auditorium, High Gallery and Tower 5, Mezzanine.

Building volume signage would appear wall mounted next to entrance. Floor/ramp identification is part of the ordinance signage that appears outside of the elevators.

AMENITIES SIGNAGE — For example: Restrooms

These would be door mounted and incorporate the international symbols where appropriate

SERVICES — For example: Admissions, Coat check.

A building plan of the Solomon R. Guggenheim Museum prepared by the architectural company, Gwathmey Siegel, Associates.

SOLOMON R. GUGGENHEIM MUSEUM
AUSTRALIA 1991
CD:Pamela L. Myers
AD,D:Colin Rowan

STATISTICAL
TABLES & GRAPHS

CHARTS & SCORES

MAPS

ARCHITECTURAL
PLANS & DRAWINGS

INSTRUCTIONAL DIAGRAMS
FOR PRODUCTS

SCIENTIFIC
ILLUSTRATIONS

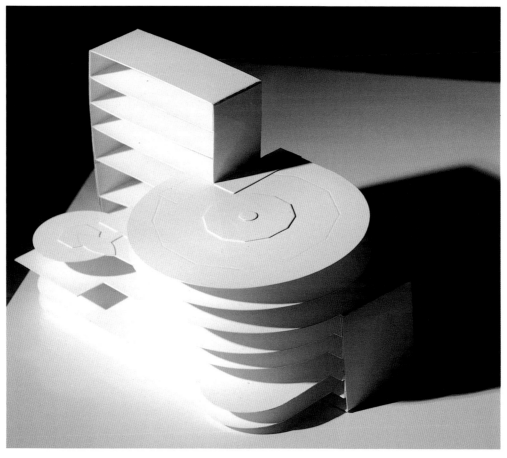

3-D diagram of the Solomon R. Guggenheim Museum showing the correspondence between volume and floor space.

ソロモン・R・グッゲンハイム美術館の床面積と建築物の容積との関係を示す立体ダイアグラム。

STATISTICAL
TABLES & GRAPHS

CHARTS & SCORES

MAPS

ARCHITECTURAL
PLANS & DRAWINGS

INSTRUCTIONAL DIAGRAMS
FOR PRODUCTS

SCIENTIFIC
ILLUSTRATIONS

THE SCIENCE MUSEUM, LONDON
ENGLAND 1991
CD:Sally Mcintosh
AD,D,I:Stuart Green
I:Barry Brocklebank
DF:Communication by Design

ロンドン科学博物館内部に新設される教育センターの間取り図。

Reception and Assembly

Schools Entrance

Cloakroom and Picnic Area

Toilets

Store

Teaching Resources and Auxiliaries

Shops

Teaching Theatres

'Lift Off' exhibition area

Plan of the Education Centre

Floor plan showing the area within the existing Science Museum, London to be developed as a new Education Center.
ロンドン科学博物館内部に新設される教育センターの間取り図。

STATISTICAL
TABLES & GRAPHS

CHARTS & SCORES

MAPS

ARCHITECTURAL
PLANS & DRAWINGS

INSTRUCTIONAL DIAGRAMS
FOR PRODUCTS

SCIENTIFIC
ILLUSTRATIONS

ESSEL'S AMUSEMENT PARK(S) INDIA LTD.
INDIA 1989
AD,D:Sudarshan Dheer
I:Narendra Vaidya
DF:Graphic Communication Concepts

General Signs Indicators

43 Control Tower
44 Gift Shop
45 Train Station
46 Exchange/Bank
47 Post Office
First Aid
Headquarters
Information
Lost and Found
Baggage Deposit
Prams
Wheel Chair
Snacks
Tickets
Toilets
Meeting Points
Telephone
Drinking Water
Rest Place
Pregnant Ladies Prohibited
Heart Patients Prohibited

Guide Map of Fun Park
ESSELWORLD

Gorai Creek

Gorai Creek

Special Notice:
Rights of admission reserved. Patrons using various rides and facilities in ESSELWORLD will do so with due notice of the various warnings displayed at appropriate places and besides that they shall so use such facilities as rides at their own risk and the management shall not owe any responsibility for mishap or any other damages.

Guide map using pictographs and signs to outline the facilities of Essel's Amusement Park in India.
インド・エッセル遊園地の施設をピクトグラムやサインで表した案内図。

NATIONS BANK
USA 1991
AD:Lowell Williams
D:Bill Carson
I:Andy Dearwater
DF:Pentagram Design Ltd.

STATISTICAL
TABLES & GRAPHS

CHARTS & SCORES

MAPS

ARCHITECTURAL
PLANS & DRAWINGS

INSTRUCTIONAL DIAGRAMS
FOR PRODUCTS

SCIENTIFIC
ILLUSTRATIONS

Part of the floor plan for a high-rise building, Nations Bank Plaza, in Atlanta. From a promotional pamphlet.
プロモーション用パンフレットより、アトランタの高層ビル「ネイションズ・バンクプラザ」のフロアープランの一部。

STATISTICAL
TABLES & GRAPHS

CHARTS & SCORES

MAPS

ARCHITECTURAL
PLANS & DRAWINGS

INSTRUCTIONAL DIAGRAMS
FOR PRODUCTS

SCIENTIFIC
ILLUSTRATIONS

CIRCUS CIRCUS ENTERPRISES, INC.
USA 1989
CD,AD,D:Don Kano
I:Carlos Delgado
DF:Kano Design Group

Diagrams showing the three levels of entertainment at Excalibur Hotel and Casino in Las Vegas, Nevada.
The illustrations were printed on translucent vellum with each level depicted and explained on separate sheets. From a Circus Circus Enterprises Inc. annual report.
サーカス・サーカス・エンタープライズ社のアニュアルリポートより、ネバダ州ラスベガスのエクスカリバーホテル＆カジノの3フロアの娯楽施設を表した図。
イラストレーションは半透明のベラム紙、フロア図は台紙に描き解説を加えてある。

JOHN PORTMAN COMPANIES
USA 1991
AD:Lowell Williams
D:Bill Carson
I:Andy Dearwater
DF:Pentagram Design Ltd.

STATISTICAL
TABLES & GRAPHS

CHARTS & SCORES

MAPS

ARCHITECTURAL
PLANS & DRAWINGS

INSTRUCTIONAL DIAGRAMS
FOR PRODUCTS

SCIENTIFIC
ILLUSTRATIONS

STATISTICAL
TABLES & GRAPHS

CHARTS & SCORES

MAPS

ARCHITECTURAL
PLANS & DRAWINGS

INSTRUCTIONAL DIAGRAMS
FOR PRODUCTS

SCIENTIFIC
ILLUSTRATIONS

Elevation and site plan of a high-rise building, One Peachtree Center, in Atlanta. From a promotional pamphlet.
プロモーション用パンフレットより、アトランタの高層ビル「ワンピーチツリー・センター」の立面図、及び平面図。

VERLAG DAS BESTE
GERMANY 1985
CD:Rudi Schmidt
AD,I:Achim Kiel
DF:Pencil Corporate Art

STATISTICAL
TABLES & GRAPHS

CHARTS & SCORES

MAPS

ARCHITECTURAL
PLANS & DRAWINGS

INSTRUCTIONAL DIAGRAMS
FOR PRODUCTS

SCIENTIFIC
ILLUSTRATIONS

古代埋葬場の規模、構造、及び配置などを示す考古学的発掘の図解。

Diagrams of archaeological excavations showing the structure, proportions and lay-out of ancient burial sites.
古代埋葬場の規模、構造、及び配置などを示す考古学的発掘の図解。

製品

いわゆる絵画と図解の違いは、絵画が多分に作者の心情を反映した「描写」的性格を重
んじるのに対して、図解は、客観的な事実の冷静な「記述」としての性格を重んじる点に
ある。

本章で紹介する製品イラストレーションと、次章で紹介する科学イラストレーションは
いずれも、こうした記述的意図をもって描かれた作品である。

本来、ダイアグラムとは、図と文字情報の共同による図解作品を指すもので、これらの
イラストレーションの中には、画面中に文字情報を含まず、厳密な意味でのダイアグラム
の範疇には属さない作品も含まれている。が、これらの作品に一貫して見られる記述的な
意図というものは、その基本的な精神をダイアグラムと共有するものといえる。

製品イラストレーションは、文字通り、製品の仕上がり、ないしは構造を図解したもの
である。同じ用途に写真が使われることも多いが、製品を美しく見せる理想的なライティ
ングや、細部の徹底した描写には、逆に「写真のように」精緻なイラストレーションの方
が威力を発揮するケースというのが珍しくない。一般的な印象とは逆に、写真というメデ
ィアは細部の写実的な描写においては、ライティング、ピント、さらには被写体の仕上が
りやコンディションと、実に多くの不確定要因が関わってくる分だけ、確実性に欠ける部
分がある。その点、人間の手で細部を徹底的に吟味、修正しながら描けるイラストレーシ
ョンは、描き手の技量さえ確かであれば、はるかに確実な結果を期待できることになる。
加えて、製品の内部構造を示す断面図等においては、イラストレーションの表現力が断然
まさっていることはいうまでもない。

これらのイラストレーションは、ある意味では一般の絵画をも上回る絵画技術を駆使し
つつも、いわゆる絵画的な詩情を排した独特の知的な美学を示している点で、視覚表現ジ
ャンルに特異な位置を占めている。

各時代の科学イラストレーションが、各時代の科学の状況を物語る貴重な視覚的証言で
あるのと同じように、製品イラストレーションは、産業革命以降の工業生産品に彩られた
消費生活史を未来に保存する、貴重きわまりない視覚素材ということができるだろう。

INSTRUCTIONAL
DIAGRAMS
FOR PRODUCTS

INSTRUCTIONAL DIAGRAMS

FOR PRODUCTS

制品 イラストレーション

The difference between fine art and illustration is that the former essentially reflects the artist's feelings and thoughts, whereas the function of the latter is the disinterested observation and recording of visual facts. The product illustrations introduced in this chapter and the scientific illustrations in the next chapter are art-works produced with just such a cool, descriptive intention.

Originally, the word "diagram" generally referred to illustrations which incorporate both graphic and text information. Among the illustrations introduced here, there are some which do not include any text. Strictly speaking, perhaps, they do not belong in the category of diagrams as it is normally defined. I dare say, however, that the intention to visually describe something from an objective viewpoint is certainly present, so these illustrations do have the essential spirit of diagrams.

A product illustration is, literally, an illustration of a finished product. It is not unusual to use photos for the same purpose, but it is often the case that a "photo-graphically correct" illustration is more effective than a real photograph. In photo-graphy, the ideal lighting, which would show the beauty of the product and, at the same time, reveal it in all its detail, can be difficult to achieve. Contrary to the com-mon assumption, photography is not always a visually reliable medium. When trying to reproduce details in photography, realism depends upon lighting, focus, the fin-ish of the subject and a number of other factors, not all of which can be controlled by the photographer.

An illustration, on the other hand, can be produced very painstakingly, highlighting each detail as necessary. Control here depends upon human doggedness so that if the artist has certain level of technique, you can always expect a high quality illus-tration. Moreover, illustrations often have greater visual impact than photos, and are infinitely superior when it comes to cross-section views, exposing internal struc-tures. This type of illustration is a genre in itself, in that it employs techniques which, in some ways, surpass those used in painting. It possesses a unique and intelligent esthetic, from which artistic or poetic sentiment has been banished.

Scientific illustrations are artifacts as well, bearing eloquent witness to the level of scientific advance in the era recorded. Product illustrations too, are extremely valu-able visual documents which tell the story of consumerism and quality of life through the evolution of products manufactured since the industrial revolution.

STATISTICAL
TABLES & GRAPHS

CHARTS & SCORES

MAPS

ARCHITECTURAL
PLANS & DRAWINGS

INSTRUCTIONAL DIAGRAMS
FOR PRODUCTS

SCIENTIFIC
ILLUSTRATIONS

P + O
ITALY 1990
CD,AD:Barbara Nerozzi
DF:Fincantieri Technical Studio

Spacial study of the axonometrics of the Crown Princess engine room. From GB progetti Magazine No. 3/4 1990.
「GB progetti マガジン」1990年3/4号より、クラウンプリンセスのエンジンルームのアクソノメトリック・スケッチ。

STATISTICAL
TABLES & GRAPHS

CHARTS & SCORES

MAPS

ARCHITECTURAL
PLANS & DRAWINGS

INSTRUCTIONAL DIAGRAMS
FOR PRODUCTS

SCIENTIFIC
ILLUSTRATIONS

HI-SHEAR INDUSTRIES, INC.
USA 1991
CD:Stephen Ferrari
D:Janet Scanlon
I:Steve Lyons
DF:The Graphic Expression, Inc.

HI-SHEAR'S STRONG COMPETITIVE POSITION RESULTS FROM ITS DESIGN AND MANUFACTURING EXPERTISE, ITS REPUTATION FOR SUPPLYING HIGH-QUALITY PRODUCTS, ITS HIGHLY PROFESSIONAL FIELD SERVICE AND ITS CONTINUING EMPHASIS ON PRODUCT INNOVATION.

1 MOST HI-LOK PINS ARE PRODUCED FROM TITANIUM ALLOY WIRE WHICH IS DRAWN, HEATED AND THEN FORGED BY THIS HEADING MACHINE INTO SLIGHTLY OVERSIZED BLANKS.

2 FOLLOWING TRIMMING, HEAT TREATMENT AND GRINDING TO EXTREMELY CLOSE TOLERANCES, THE "FILLET" AREA BETWEEN THE HEAD AND CYLIN-DRICAL BODY OF THE PIN IS COLD-WORKED BETWEEN HARDENED DIES TO IMPROVE ITS FATIGUE LIFE.

3 WARMED TO SEVERAL HUNDRED DEGREES FAHRENHEIT, THE PIN THREADS ARE FORMED BY ROLLING THE BLANK BETWEEN FLAT DIES.

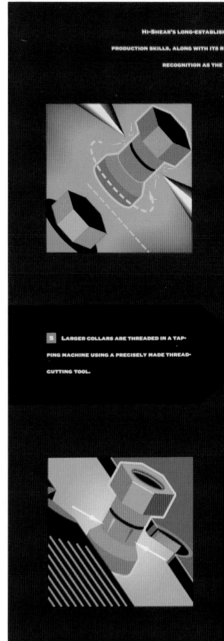

HI-SHEAR'S LONG-ESTABLISHI PRODUCTION SKILLS, ALONG WITH ITS RIC RECOGNITION AS THE I

5 LARGER COLLARS ARE THREADED IN A TAP-PING MACHINE USING A PRECISELY MADE THREAD-CUTTING TOOL.

STATISTICAL
TABLES & GRAPHS

CHARTS & SCORES

MAPS

ARCHITECTURAL
PLANS & DRAWINGS

INSTRUCTIONAL DIAGRAMS
FOR PRODUCTS

SCIENTIFIC
ILLUSTRATIONS

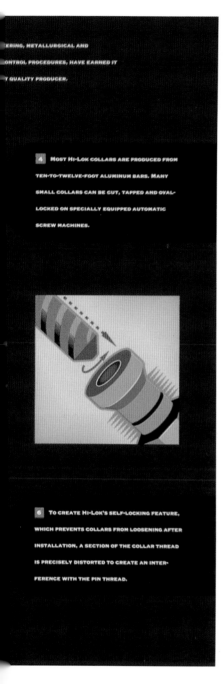

ERING, METALLURGICAL AND
CONTROL PROCEDURES, HAVE EARNED IT
Y QUALITY PRODUCER.

4 MOST HI-LOK COLLARS ARE PRODUCED FROM
TEN-TO-TWELVE-FOOT ALUMINUM BARS. MANY
SMALL COLLARS CAN BE CUT, TAPPED AND OVAL-
LOCKED ON SPECIALLY EQUIPPED AUTOMATIC
SCREW MACHINES.

6 TO CREATE HI-LOK'S SELF-LOCKING FEATURE,
WHICH PREVENTS COLLARS FROM LOOSENING AFTER
INSTALLATION, A SECTION OF THE COLLAR THREAD
IS PRECISELY DISTORTED TO CREATE AN INTER-
FERENCE WITH THE PIN THREAD.

HI-SHEAR OFFERS MORE THAN 30 PRODUCT LINES WHICH HAVE BEEN DESIGNED INTO
COMMERCIAL AND MILITARY AIRCRAFT PRODUCED BY VIRTUALLY EVERY MAJOR MANUFACTURER
AS WELL AS SPACE VEHICLES INCLUDING THE SPACE SHUTTLE.

7 PINS AND COLLARS ARE HEAT TREATED AT
VARIOUS STAGES OF THE MANUFACTURING PROCESS
TO DEVELOP THE EXCEPTIONAL STRENGTH RE-
QUIRED FOR THEIR SPECIALIZED USE.

8 TITANIUM PINS ARE OFTEN FINISHED WITH
HI-KOTE 1, A PROPRIETARY COATING WHICH
PROTECTS THE AIRFRAME STRUCTURE FROM COR-
ROSION. SPECIALIZED COATINGS AND FINISHING
TREATMENTS ARE APPLIED TO PINS AND COLLARS.

9 FINISHED PINS AND COLLARS ARE SUBJECTED
TO EXTENSIVE TESTING INCLUDING VERIFICATION
OF STRENGTH, CONFORMANCE TO CUSTOMER-
MANDATED SPECIFICATIONS AND A VARIETY OF TEN-
SION, SHEAR AND FATIGUE TESTS.

Diagrams of various manufacturing steps as part of an overall quality process. From a Hi-Shear Industries Inc. annual report.
ハイシアー・インダストリーズ社のアニュアルリポートより、製品の全体的な品質管理過程を表すために紹介された、いくつかの製造過程図。

STATISTICAL
TABLES & GRAPHS

CHARTS & SCORES

MAPS

ARCHITECTURAL
PLANS & DRAWINGS

INSTRUCTIONAL DIAGRAMS
FOR PRODUCTS

SCIENTIFIC
ILLUSTRATIONS

HI-SHEAR INDUSTRIES, INC.
USA 1986
CD:Stephen Ferrari
I:Ron Scott
DF:The Graphic Expression, Inc.

STATISTICAL
TABLES & GRAPHS

CHARTS & SCORES

MAPS

ARCHITECTURAL
PLANS & DRAWINGS

INSTRUCTIONAL DIAGRAMS
FOR PRODUCTS

SCIENTIFIC
ILLUSTRATIONS

Illustration utilizing computer modeling to display the company's range of products. From a Hi-Shear Industries Inc. annual report.
ハイシアー・インダストリーズ社のアニュアルリポートより、会社の製品の適用範囲をコンピューター・モデリングを使って表すイラストレーション。

STATISTICAL
TABLES & GRAPHS

CHARTS & SCORES

MAPS

ARCHITECTURAL
PLANS & DRAWINGS

INSTRUCTIONAL DIAGRAMS
FOR PRODUCTS

SCIENTIFIC
ILLUSTRATIONS

Isometric assembly of Eco-iD "Evolution" freestanding structure which can be extended and reduced as required.
必要に応じて伸縮自在な家具システム「Eco-iDエボリューション」のアイソメトリック組立図。

STATISTICAL
TABLES & GRAPHS

CHARTS & SCORES

MAPS

ARCHITECTURAL
PLANS & DRAWINGS

INSTRUCTIONAL DIAGRAMS
FOR PRODUCTS

SCIENTIFIC
ILLUSTRATIONS

THE KNOLL GROUP
USA 1990
AD:Alison Choate
I:Alan Kikuchi
DF:The Knoll Group

This "exploded view" of a Bulldog chair reveals details that are normally not visible and gives an understanding of how some of the many unique parts fit together.
「ブルドッグチェア」分解組立図。通常見えない部分を見せ、数多くの特殊な部品がどのように組み合わさっているかを解説している。

MATSUSHITA ELECTRIC
INDUSTRIAL CO., LTD.
JAPAN 1991
CD:Mikio Mori
AD:Masato Okazaki
I:Takatoshi Oki

STATISTICAL
TABLES & GRAPHS

CHARTS & SCORES

MAPS

ARCHITECTURAL
PLANS & DRAWINGS

INSTRUCTIONAL DIAGRAMS
FOR PRODUCTS

SCIENTIFIC
ILLUSTRATIONS

Technics CD player technical illustration. From a Matsushita Electric Industrial sales catalogue.
松下電機産業の製品カタログより、「テクニクスCDプレイヤー」のテクニカル・イラストレーション。

PIONEER ELECTRIC CORPORATION

JAPAN

CD:Isao Kobayashi

AD:Yukio Sekido

D:Masakatsu Nakamura

I:Ryo Ohshita

SONY CORPORATION

JAPAN

DF:Sony Corporation Advertising & Marketing

Communication Strategy Group

STATISTICAL
TABLES & GRAPHS

CHARTS & SCORES

MAPS

ARCHITECTURAL
PLANS & DRAWINGS

INSTRUCTIONAL DIAGRAMS
FOR PRODUCTS

SCIENTIFIC
ILLUSTRATIONS

Illustration of the turntable unit in a CD player "PD-T07".

From a Pioneer Electric Corporation sales catalogue.

パイオニア社の製品カタログより、CDプレイヤー「PD-T07」のターンテーブル部のイラストレーション。

Diagram showing the internal structure of a color television "Kirara Basso".

From a Sony Corporation sales catalogue.

ソニー社の製品カタログより、カラーテレビ「キララ・バッソ」の内部構造図。

STATISTICAL
TABLES & GRAPHS

CHARTS & SCORES

MAPS

ARCHITECTURAL
PLANS & DRAWINGS

INSTRUCTIONAL DIAGRAMS
FOR PRODUCTS

SCIENTIFIC
ILLUSTRATIONS

Illustration of the Zanussi ZTD900 washing machine, manufactured by Zanussi Elettrodomestici spa. in Italy. From MODO magazine #137.
「モードマガジン」137号より、イタリアのザヌッシ電気機器社の「ザヌッシZTD900洗濯機」のイラストレーション。

STATISTICAL
TABLES & GRAPHS

CHARTS & SCORES

MAPS

ARCHITECTURAL
PLANS & DRAWINGS

INSTRUCTIONAL DIAGRAMS
FOR PRODUCTS

SCIENTIFIC
ILLUSTRATIONS

HITACHI SALES CORPORATION
JAPAN 1989
D:Yoshiaki Yonejima

Illustration explaining the operating procedure for a home appliance dish washer/dryer "Arattokuwa". From a Hitachi Sales Corporation catalogue.
日立家電社の製品カタログより、家庭用食器洗い乾燥器「洗っとくわ」の操作手順の解説イラストレーション。

EUNOS INC.
JAPAN 1990
CD:Kazutomo Kanazawa
AD:Hiroyuki Fukusato
D:Mitsugu Muramatsu
I:Takashi Ohno/Takeshi Hosokawa

STATISTICAL
TABLES & GRAPHS

CHARTS & SCORES

MAPS

ARCHITECTURAL
PLANS & DRAWINGS

INSTRUCTIONAL DIAGRAMS
FOR PRODUCTS

SCIENTIFIC
ILLUSTRATIONS

STATISTICAL
TABLES & GRAPHS

CHARTS & SCORES

MAPS

ARCHITECTURAL
PLANS & DRAWINGS

INSTRUCTIONAL DIAGRAMS
FOR PRODUCTS

SCIENTIFIC
ILLUSTRATIONS

Illustrations of the engine and the chassis of the Eunos Cosmo automobile. From a Eunos Inc. sales catalogue.
ユーノス社の製品カタログより、自動車「ユーノス・コスモ」のエンジン部、及びシャーシ部のイラストレーション。

STATISTICAL
TABLES & GRAPHS

CHARTS & SCORES

MAPS

ARCHITECTURAL
PLANS & DRAWINGS

INSTRUCTIONAL DIAGRAMS
FOR PRODUCTS

SCIENTIFIC
ILLUSTRATIONS

LOCKHEED CORPORATION
USA 1992
CD,AD:Carl Seltzer
D:Luis Alvarado
I:Jim Speas
DF:Carl Seltzer Design Office

STATISTICAL
TABLES & GRAPHS

CHARTS & SCORES

MAPS

ARCHITECTURAL
PLANS & DRAWINGS

INSTRUCTIONAL DIAGRAMS
FOR PRODUCTS

SCIENTIFIC
ILLUSTRATIONS

The F-117 Stealth Fighter rose to worldwide fame during the Gulf War,
but this was the first time the U.S. Government permitted a cutaway view of this historic but once top-secret aircraft.
湾岸戦争で世界中の脚光を浴びた「F-117ステルス戦闘機」の断面図。かつては最高機密に属したこの戦闘機の内部の公開を合衆国政府が許可したのは初めてのことである。

STATISTICAL
TABLES & GRAPHS

CHARTS & SCORES

MAPS

ARCHITECTURAL
PLANS & DRAWINGS

INSTRUCTIONAL DIAGRAMS
FOR PRODUCTS

SCIENTIFIC
ILLUSTRATIONS

Illustration of a Jaguar automobile used on the package of a plastic model.
プラモデルのパッケージに印刷された、自動車「ジャガー」のイラストレーション。

イラストレーション

科学

科学イラストレーションの歴史は古い。

古代の天文図から、中世の化学図解、ルネッサンスの解剖図、そして近世以降の種々の科学書を飾る図解群は、そのまま科学という名の人間のあくなき探求心の足取りの、視覚化されたものといえる。

医学図解、天文図解、地学図解等が、科学イラストレーションの代表であるが、こうしたテーマやジャンルを問わず、なんらかの現象や知識を客観的かつ科学的な関心のもとに描いた図解作品はすべて、広い意味での科学イラストレーションに含まれると考えていいだろう。

もともと、絵画というものは、描かれた対象を視覚的に所有するための道具としての性格が強いものであった。したがって、人間は常に、自分が「欲しい」と思うものを描き続けてきたのである。原始時代、それは狩りの獲物であり、中世、それは神の恩寵であり、ルネッサンス期、それは理想的な人間像であった。

それぞれの動機は、それぞれに呪術、宗教、人文主義などと別の名前で呼ばれてはいるが、それらはすべて、なんらかのかたちで欲しいもの、手に入れたいものを描いているという点において共通している。

科学イラストレーションも例外ではない。それらの画面は、ある意味では、人間が「欲しい」と思うものの筆頭に挙げられるべき、知識というものへの思いの視覚化に他ならないのである。

したがって、科学イラストレーションの制作にあたっては、精緻な観察眼と確かな描画技術もさることながら、なにより、読者の知的関心の代理人あるいは読者の眼の代理人としての、好奇心に裏付けられた創造性というものが要求される。

近年、著しい発達を遂げたコンピュータ・グラフィックスなどは、かつて人間の手では決して描くことのできなかった画像を次々に実現してみせているわけだが、こうした描画技術の飛躍的な発展に直面するほどに、ダイアグラム・デザイナーは、この技術に見合うだけの、好奇心とイマジネーションというものを要求されることになるのである。

SCIENTIFIC
ILLUSTRATIONS

SCIENTIFIC ILLUSTRATIONS

The history of scientific illustrations goes back further than you might think. In Medieval times there were already astronomical and chemical illustrations. Later came the anatomical illustrations of the Renaissance period and, of course, ever more sophisticated illustrations have been appearing in various scientific publications since the beginning of the modern age. These are a direct reflection of the history of the human desire for knowledge, called science. When we talk about scientific illustration, we immediately think of medical drawings, geological diagrams and so forth. Regardless of theme or subject matter, however, if an illustration objectively depicts a certain phenomenon or body of knowledge with scientific interest, then, at least in the broader sense, it can be called a scientific illustration.

Originally, paintings functioned, in a visual sense, as a tool to take possession of the object depicted. Just as early humans made cave paintings of the animals they wanted to capture or kill, so people have always depicted the object of their desire. In the Medieval age it was God's love, and during the Renaissance it was the ideal image of man. The motivation for creating those images is not dissimilar to that of magical incantations, whether it is called religion, humanism, or something else, we depict what we want in order to call it forth.

Scientific illustrations are no exception; these images are the very visualization of the love of knowledge which has characterized the modern age. In producing a scientific illustration, creativity is driven by curiosity as the agent. The viewer's intellectual capacity is engaged and the reader's critical eye is assumed to be very sharp. Thus, for the designer, great powers of observation are required and a sure technique of rendering it in accurate detail. In this field, as in others, computer graphics have made a spectacular contribution and are embraced enthusiastically by most artists. Images now are being realized which, until recently, would have been difficult even to imagine, much less achieve. Diagram designers are facing quantum leaps in imaging technique and potential, but this does not necessarily make the job easier. Indeed, his artist's curiosity and imagination may be more challenged than ever by these exciting new tools.

科学
イラストレーション

ROCHE PRODUCTS LIMITED
ENGLAND 1971
CD,AD,D:Mervyn Kurlansky
D:Maddy Bennet
DF:Pentagram Design Ltd.

SCHOOL OF
VISUAL ARTS COMPUTER ILLUSTRATION PROJECT
USA 1991
I:Frank Fasano

STATISTICAL
TABLES & GRAPHS

CHARTS & SCORES

MAPS

ARCHITECTURAL
PLANS & DRAWINGS

INSTRUCTIONAL DIAGRAMS
FOR PRODUCTS

SCIENTIFIC
ILLUSTRATIONS

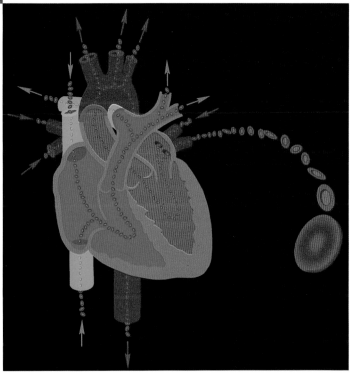

Illustration showing the main sensory pathway to the cortex indicated by arrows.
From a Roche Products Limited promotional brochure for a new tranquillizer.
ロッシュ・プロダクツ社の新精神安定剤プロモーション用パンフレットより、
大脳皮質への感覚の到達経路を矢印で示すイラストレーション。

Illustration of a heart with blood flow.
血液の循環経路を示す心臓のイラストレーション。

AMERICAN HEALTH PARTNERS, INC.
USA 1987
AD:Will Hopkins/Ira Friedlander
D,I:Peter Bradford
I:Frank H. Netter
DF:Peter Bradford & Associates

STATISTICAL
TABLES & GRAPHS

CHARTS & SCORES

MAPS

ARCHITECTURAL
PLANS & DRAWINGS

INSTRUCTIONAL DIAGRAMS
FOR PRODUCTS

SCIENTIFIC
ILLUSTRATIONS

*O'Shea got to the
hospital an hour after
his symptoms began.*

the edge of the bed for a few minutes,
the pain stopped. But it returned when
he resumed his shower. And this time,
it didn't go away.

Alarmed, O'Shea called a friend in
his parish and together they drove to
Seton Medical Center a few miles
south in Daly City. They arrived at the
emergency room a little more than an
hour after his symptoms had begun.
Cardiologist Colman Ryan needed only
one look at O'Shea's electrocardio-
gram to determine he was in the mid-
dle of a heart attack.

But there was still time to stop it.
First, Dr. Ryan sent O'Shea down to
the cardiac catheterization lab for a
coronary angiogram, an X-ray study
done with contrast dye injected
through a catheter into the coronary
arteries. The angiogram would reveal
the precise location of the blockage
and how extensive it was. The cardiol-
ogists could then try to unclog the artery and halt the attack.

Then Ryan beeped Dr. Richard Myler, one of the country's foremost ex-
perts in balloon angioplasty (also called
percutaneous transluminal coronary
angioplasty, or PTCA). Myler, who's
on staff at the hospital, had had success using PTCA as an emergency
measure to stop a heart attack in progress. (Normally, the procedure is
used to open vessels that are nar-
rowed but not completely closed, in
patients who aren't acutely ill.)

O'Shea's angiogram results came
in: The clot had completely blocked
the left anterior descending artery,
which supplies blood to the front of the
heart and to the wall that divides the
two beating chambers.

Ryan alerted an open-heart surgery
team in case emergency bypass surgery was needed. In emergency bypass, an arterial graft is used to detour

46

**During a heart
attack, a clot
blocks blood
circulation to
part of the
heart muscle.
Affected areas
die from insuf-
ficient oxygen
supply. Three
new methods
permit doctors
to restore
blood flow, and
thus cut short a
heart attack
and limit dam-
age. Clockwise:
TPA and other
clot-busting
drugs dissolve
the blockage;
in angioplasty,
a catheter is
snaked through
an artery to the
site and an
inflated bal-
loon at its tip
breaks up the
clot; emergency
bypass detours
blood supply
around the
obstruction.**

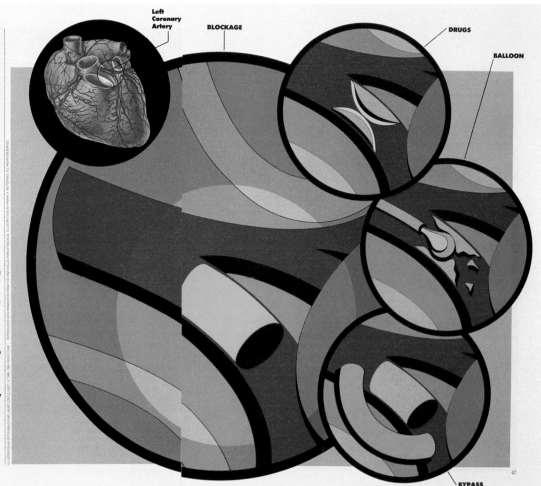

Left
Coronary
Artery

BLOCKAGE

DRUGS

BALLOON

BYPASS

47

Illustration of three methods to restore blood flow to the heart and limit heart attack damage. From American Health magazine.
「アメリカン・ヘルスマガジン」より、心臓への血液の流入を修復しながら心臓発作による損傷を抑える3つの方法を解説したイラストレーション。

ACCESS PRESS, INC.

USA 1988

AD:Richard Saul Wurman

D,I:Lorraine Christiani

D:Peter Bradford

I:Michael Everitt

DF:Peter Bradford & Associates

STATISTICAL TABLES & GRAPHS

CHARTS & SCORES

MAPS

ARCHITECTURAL PLANS & DRAWINGS

INSTRUCTIONAL DIAGRAMS FOR PRODUCTS

SCIENTIFIC ILLUSTRATIONS

63

FACE NERVE
RHIZOTOMY, CUTTING OF THE TRIGEMINAL NERVE

101,000 Frequency in 1982 **2-3 hrs** Duration of Operation

Nature of problem.

Trigeminal neuralgia, or tic douloureux, is a condition in which intense shooting or stabbing pain occurs on one side of the face. In the early stage, the episodes last no more than 1 or 2 minutes, with pain-free periods lasting for months. Later, the pain-free intervals become shorter. The pain follows the path of 1 of the cranial nerves; however, the cause of the condition remains unknown. The elective surgery to cut the nerve, **rhizotomy**, will bring relief.

Frequency. Just under 70 percent of all patients are women. Slightly less than half of all patients are between the ages of 45 and 64.

Surgical preparation.

The diagnosis can usually be made on the basis of your symptoms, together with the absence of any other demonstrable cause of the pain, such as a recent head injury or the presence of a tumor. To confirm the diagnosis, you may undergo a **Cat scan** of the head or a nuclear scan of the brain to determine if a tumor is present.

In conjunction with hospital admission, you may also undergo the following tests: **Complete blood count, SMA, Urinalysis, Chest x-ray** and **EKG.**

When you are admitted to the hospital, you will be examined by a physician. Because the doctor will pay special attention to the *neurological* aspects of the exam, he or she will assess the function of each of your *cranial nerves.* You will be asked to smile, show your teeth, wrinkle your forehead, etc. About an hour before surgery, you will be given a sedative by injection. You will put on a surgical gown and socks, and an intravenous line will be started in your hand or forearm. The area near the incision will be shaved.

Anesthetic. You will receive a general gas anesthetic, preceded by an intravenous anesthetic.

Procedure.

1 The surgeon makes a diagonal incision running from a point in front of the top of the ear to just near the crown and above the ear.

2 A small hinge-like flap of bone and dura (the covering of the brain) is cut to temporarily expose the operative site. An operating microscope is used to identify the *trigeminal* ganglion, a bundle of nerves which transmits information between the brain and 3 areas of the face.

3 The *rootlets* (connectors of the sensory nerve to the ganglion) are cut.

Stages of recovery.

You remain in the recovery room 1 to 3 hours. On the first postoperative day, you will probably be allowed to sit in a chair.

Limitations. You will have to wear a rather flamboyant, turban-style dressing until your incision has healed. It will take time for your hair to regrow.

Drugs. You will be given oral painkiller to relieve discomfort at the point where the hinge-like flap was created.

Complications. Complications are rare following this surgery; however there is the possibility that a small **hematoma** will form in the line of the closed incision.

Scar. The operation will leave you with a short diagonal scar from just in front of the ear to a point above the ear on the side of the head near the crown. As your hair grows back, the scar will be all but totally obscured.

The flap of bone and dura is then replaced over the site and the skin is sutured.

91

KNEE CARTILAGE
ARTHROSCOPY, EXCISION OF SEMILUNAR CARTILAGE OF THE KNEE

155,000 Frequency in 1982 **1 hr** Duration of Operation

Nature of problem.

The most highly publicized causes of torn knee cartilage are sports injuries, but the cartilage can be damaged in other strenuous activities, such as ballet dancing. If the pain becomes severe and limits the range of motion in your knee, the damaged cartilage can be removed. It is considered elective surgery.

Frequency. Over 70 percent of all patients are men, mostly between the ages of 15 and 44.

*Arthroscopy may also be used as a diagnostic tool. A slender metal tube with a self-contained light source is inserted in a joint (knee, ankle or shoulder) allowing the doctor to detect torn cartilage or tendons and to assess the severity of arthritis. It can be done with local anesthetic in a doctor's office. Some doctors prefer to diagnose knee problems with an **arthrogram.** the knee is numbed with a local anesthetic and then air or contrast dye is injected into the joint. The joint is moved while fluoroscopic pictures (x-ray movies) are taken. The dye helps your doctor distinguish between the small overlapping structures inside the joint that don't show up well on conventional x-rays.*

Surgical preparation.

Before you are admitted to the hospital, you will have **x-rays** taken of your knee to show any bony abnormalities and possibly an **Arthrogram** which involves a dye injection to view muscle, ligament and cartilage tissue inside the joint. In addition, you will probably have a **Complete blood count, Blood clotting tests,** a **Urinalysis,** and a **Chest x-ray.** If you are over 40, you probably will have an **EKG.**

About an hour before the surgery, you will receive a sedative by injection. You will dress in a surgical cap, gown and socks.

Anesthetic. The surgeon will inject your knee with a local anesthetic.

Procedure.

1 The surgeon makes a short incision over the damaged *meniscus,* the crescent-shaped cartilage on the sides of the knee cap. The incision may be either *lateral* (on the outer side of the joint), or *medial* (inner side), depending on the injury. Through the incision, the physician introduces an arthroscope, permitting him or her to see the extent of the damage.

2 With cutting instruments inserted in the arthroscope, the damaged cartilage is removed.

View from top

3 After closure, heavily padded dressing is applied.

knee cap

damaged lateral meniscus

damaged cartilage

Stages of recovery.

Limitations. Because your knee will remain sore and stiff for some time, you probably won't need to be warned not to run, jump or engage in strenuous exercise or competitive sports for several weeks. Your stitches will be removed after about 2 weeks. Then your doctor probably will have you begin an exercise program to regain strength.

Drugs. There will be some pain, but it usually can be controlled with oral medication.

Complications. There are usually no complications following this procedure.

Scar. You will have a small scar where the incision is made.

There are roughly 65,000 knee implants a year. The new joint alone (not counting installation) cost about $2500 in 1985. Knee and hip joint replacements are made out of the same material used to make fan blades in jet airplanes—a cobalt, molybdenum and chromium alloy that is heated to 2800 degrees Fahrenheit before being poured into a mold.

77

BLADDER LESION
TRANSURETHRAL EXCISION OF BLADDER LESION

120,000 Frequency in 1982 **½-1½ hr** Duration of Operation

Nature of problem.

Small localized tumors of the bladder that are not deeply embedded in the bladder wall can be removed with a resectoscope. This slender tubular instrument can be inserted through the urethra; with it your doctor can see and remove tissue for analysis and evaluation. This operation is elective, in that within limits, you can choose when to have the procedure done. If a bladder tumor is present, it must be removed and evaluated.

Frequency. Of the reported bladder lesions in 1982, almost 70 percent of patients were men and more than 60 percent were over age 65.

*Bladder lesions may be more common in older men because of **stagnated fluid flow** which may be caused by prostatic disease that come naturally with age. **Smoking** is also considered a possible factor.*

Surgical preparation.

Before the decision to operate is made, you may have had several diagnostic tests including **Urinalysis** and **Cystoscopy,** a visual examination of the urethra and bladder through a fiberoptic scope similar to the one used in the operation. **Intravenous pyelography (IVP)** and **Cystography** (x-ray of the bladder) may be ordered as well. Routine testing during admission to the hospital will probably include the following: **Complete blood count, Urinalysis, Urine culture, SMA, Blood clotting tests, Chest x-ray** and **EKG.** You may be admitted to the hospital either the day before or the morning of your surgery.

About an hour before the operation, you will be given a sedative by injection. You will put on a surgical cap, gown and socks. An IV needle will be inserted into the back of your hand or your forearm for later connection to the IV line in the operating room.

Anesthetic. You will receive a spinal or general anesthetic.

Procedure.

1 A resectoscope is inserted through the urethra into the bladder.

2 With a cutting instrument fitted into the resectoscope, the tumor, along with the underlying tissue lining the bladder and muscle, is gradually cut away into fragments that can be passed out through the urethra.

3 The remaining base of the tumor is destroyed by high frequency current conducted by an instrument fitted into the resectoscope.

tumor

bladder

bladder lining

resectoscope

urethra

tumor fragments

high frequency current

Stages of recovery.

You will probably remain in the recovery room for an hour or less. (If you received a general anesthetic, you may remain there a little longer.) On the first postoperative day, you will begin walking.

Limitations. You will be instructed to avoid heavy lifting and strenuous activity for several weeks. In the first few days after surgery, you will feel a constant urge to urinate as the bladder fills. This condition subsides as the lining of your bladder heals.

Drugs. You will be given medication for postoperative pain, as well as an antibiotic to prevent infection. Your doctor may also prescribe medication to help you sleep.

Complications. If postoperative bleeding persists or is massive, you will return to the operating room for cystoscopic examination of the bladder. Any bleeding sites will be cauterized.

Scar. You will have no visible scar.

Illustrations for step-by-step explanations of common surgical procedure. From Medical Access Guide Book.

「メディカルアクセス・ガイドブック」より、外科手術の方法を段階をおいながら解説するイラストレーション。

STATISTICAL
TABLES & GRAPHS

CHARTS & SCORES

MAPS

ARCHITECTURAL
PLANS & DRAWINGS

INSTRUCTIONAL DIAGRAMS
FOR PRODUCTS

SCIENTIFIC
ILLUSTRATIONS

STATISTICAL
TABLES & GRAPHS

CHARTS & SCORES

MAPS

ARCHITECTURAL
PLANS & DRAWINGS

INSTRUCTIONAL DIAGRAMS
FOR PRODUCTS

SCIENTIFIC
ILLUSTRATIONS

Computer-generated image of internal organs showing the development of the intestinal tract. From the TV program, "Human Body".
TV番組「人体」より、CGによる内臓透視図、及び腸管の進化過程図。

KRAMES COMMUNICATIONS
USA 1990
AD:Fran Milner
I:John Daugherty

SMITHKLINE BEECHAM
USA 1992
AD:David Holms
I:John Daugherty
DF:Frank J. Corbett

STATISTICAL
TABLES & GRAPHS

CHARTS & SCORES

MAPS

ARCHITECTURAL
PLANS & DRAWINGS

INSTRUCTIONAL DIAGRAMS
FOR PRODUCTS

SCIENTIFIC
ILLUSTRATIONS

Cover illustration for a patient education booklet on polyps and colon cancer.
Two polyps are shown in the descending colon.
患者への教育用パンフレットより、表紙に使用されたポリープや結腸癌のイラストレーション。
傾斜する結腸に2つのポリープが見える。

Illustration promoting a leading antibiotic drug used to treat mixed bowel infections.
The illustration depicts a perforated gangrenous appendix,
a penetrating abdominal wound, ruptured diverticula,
a lower bowel obstruction and general abdominal peritonitis.
併発腸炎を治療する有力な抗生剤の広告用イラストレーション。
壊疽症、孔虫垂、貫通腹部創傷、腸閉塞、腹膜炎等が描かれている。

STATISTICAL
TABLES & GRAPHS

CHARTS & SCORES

MAPS

ARCHITECTURAL
PLANS & DRAWINGS

INSTRUCTIONAL DIAGRAMS
FOR PRODUCTS

SCIENTIFIC
ILLUSTRATIONS

Anterior view of the muscles of the human body. The illustration, showing the adult human male in a classical pose,
was used in an advertisement to promote a feeling of strength and grace.
人体の筋肉図。力強さと優美さをそなえ、古典的ポーズをとるこの成人男性のイラストレーションは広告に使用された。

STATISTICAL
TABLES & GRAPHS

CHARTS & SCORES

MAPS

ARCHITECTURAL
PLANS & DRAWINGS

INSTRUCTIONAL DIAGRAMS
FOR PRODUCTS

SCIENTIFIC
ILLUSTRATIONS

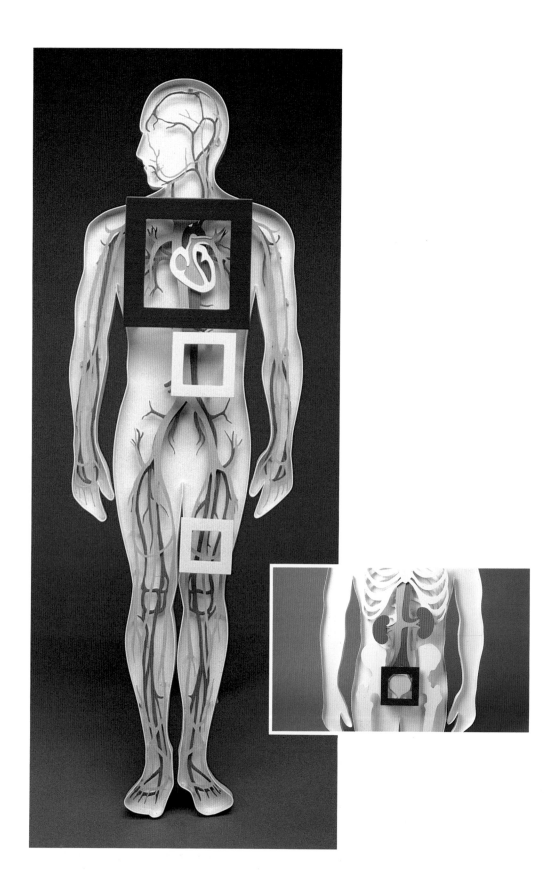

Illustration of cardiovascular system and urinary tract for Pfizer Technology Exhibit that shows pharmaceutical and hospital products.
医薬品、及び医療用品を紹介する「フィーザー社テクノロジー展」のために制作された心臓血管系と尿路の図解。

S

CHARTS & SCORES

MAPS

ARCHITECTURAL
PLANS & DRAWINGS

INSTRUCTIONAL DIAGRAMS
FOR PRODUCTS

SCIENTIFIC
ILLUSTRATIONS

Gram Negative Sepsis:
A Deadly Disease

The Clinical Picture

Fever and chills, alarmingly low blood pressure, rapid respiration, and a quickening pulse—together these signs warn of sepsis. Organ failures and biochemical changes quickly multiply, each complicating the other. Typically, doctors must treat the rapidly progressing disease before laboratory studies confirm the diagnosis. This diagram maps some of the ravages of the disease.

BRAIN. Confusion, disorientation, coma.

HEART. Pumping action falters, blood pressure drops, and blood flow to vital organs slows.

LUNGS. Adult respiratory distress syndrome, characterized by shortness of breath, impaired oxygen transfer, and fluid accumulation.

KIDNEYS. Functional failure caused by low blood pressure and vascular damage.

LIVER. Lowered production of clotting factors. Poor metabolism, resulting in jaundice.

INTESTINES. Function stops. Intestinal walls may leak, spilling more bacteria and endotoxin into the abdominal cavity.

BLOOD VESSELS. A condition called disseminated intravascular coagulation causes blood to clot along some vessels and to hemorrhage from others.

Incidence of the Disease

Gram negative sepsis is not only life-threatening, it is becoming more common. Many of the medical advances that prolong the lives of the seriously ill also leave them more vulnerable to sepsis. The incidence of sepsis in the United States has nearly tripled in the past decade. Thirty to forty percent of sepsis cases are caused by gram negative bacterial infections in the bloodstream (bacteremia). Mortality in this group can reach 60 percent.

Cases of sepsis in U.S. hospitals (in thousands)
Source: National Center for Health Statistics

6

Gram negative sepsis is a disease caused by severe infection with gram negative bacteria. This class of bacteria, which includes *Escherichia coli*, *Pseudomonas*, and *Klebsiella*, has become a leading cause of infections in hospitals. At greatest risk are the elderly, surgical patients, and persons whose immune systems have been compromised by disease or by medical treatments such as chemotherapy. ■ Under normal circumstances, gram negative bacteria live harmlessly on the skin and in the gastrointestinal tract. The body's defenses, including the immune system, usually keep the bacteria in check. When this delicate balance is disrupted, however, the bacteria can cause an invasive infection. The infection can start at many sites: along a surgical incision or a catheter, in the urinary tract, in the lungs, or in the abdominal cavity. ■ The presence of gram negative bacteria in the bloodstream (bacteremia) allows the infection to spread further. As the bacteria course through the body, they shed endotoxin, a component of their outer membranes. In many cases endotoxin starts a cascade of biochemical reactions that can result in shock, organ failure, and death—sometimes within a few hours. ■ Standard treatment includes antibiotics against bacteria, drugs to restore normal blood pressure, and often the use of life-support systems such as respirators and hemodialysis equipment. But no treatment is entirely adequate. In a recent trial 49 percent of gram negative bacteremic patients given standard treatment (without Centoxin) died within 28 days. Mortality rose to 57 percent among bacteremic patients who were in shock and to 73 percent among those in shock with organ failure.

7

Development of Centoxin

How Centoxin Works

Different types of gram negative bacteria have different endotoxins, but virtually all endotoxin molecules have a common segment known as lipid A. Centoxin works by binding to lipid A, blocking the potentially lethal chain reaction set off by endotoxin.

1. When gram negative bacteria and endotoxin reach the bloodstream in amounts that overwhelm the immune system, they are quickly carried throughout the body, causing the serious complications of sepsis.

2. Although antibiotics can successfully destroy gram negative bacteria, they are powerless against endotoxin.

3. Centoxin is infused into the bloodstream and binds to the lipid A portion of endotoxin, diminishing its lethal effects.

Endotoxin is a natural part of the outer membrane of gram negative bacteria. As the bacteria divide or die, their exterior membranes unleash endotoxin.

Some evidence suggests that even as antibiotics destroy the bacteria, still more endotoxin may be shed by the resulting rupture of cell membranes.

Centoxin is highly specific, binding only to its target, lipid A.

The quest that led to Centoxin began in the early 1970s when researchers including Dr. McCabe in Boston and Drs. Ziegler and Braude in San Diego demonstrated that the human immune system produces polyclonal antibodies in response to endotoxin. ■ Theorizing that antibodies against endotoxin might improve survival in gram negative bacteremia, Drs. Ziegler and Braude conducted a landmark study known as the J5 trial. Volunteers from the San Diego police and fire departments were vaccinated with J5, an inactivated strain of gram negative bacteria. Serum containing polyclonal antibodies against J5 was then collected from the volunteers and used to treat patients with gram negative bacteremia. The results, presented in **The New England Journal of Medicine** in 1982, showed that the J5 antiserum reduced mortality by 37 percent. ■ But the antiserum did not lend itself to commercial production. Looking for an alternative, the researchers turned to Drs. Kaplan and Teng at Stanford University, who, among others, were investigating monoclonal antibody technology. Then only a few years old, this technology held the promise of providing highly specific, pure, and uniform anti-endotoxin antibodies in commercial quantities. From the work at Stanford came the human IgM monoclonal antibody that Centocor has since formulated into the drug called Centoxin. In 1991 Dr. Ziegler and colleagues reported in **The New England Journal of Medicine** that Centoxin, like the J5 polyclonal antiserum, saved lives. During a placebo-controlled trial sponsored by Centocor, Centoxin reduced mortality in gram negative bacteremic patients by 39 percent. In cases of bacteremia and septic shock, Centoxin lowered mortality by 42 percent.

9

Diagram showing the attack of an infection on a human body and how a drug works against it. From a Centocor, Inc. annual report.
セントコア社のアニュアルリポートより、伝染病が人体を侵し、かつ医薬品がいかにそれに対処するかを表した図。

STATISTICAL
TABLES & GRAPHS

CHARTS & SCORES

MAPS

ARCHITECTURAL
PLANS & DRAWINGS

INSTRUCTIONAL DIAGRAMS
FOR PRODUCTS

SCIENTIFIC
ILLUSTRATIONS

CENTOCOR, INC.
USA 1987
CD:Charles C. Cabot Ⅲ
AD,D:Joel Katz
D,I:Dan Picard
I:Stacey Lewis
DF:Katz Wheeler Design

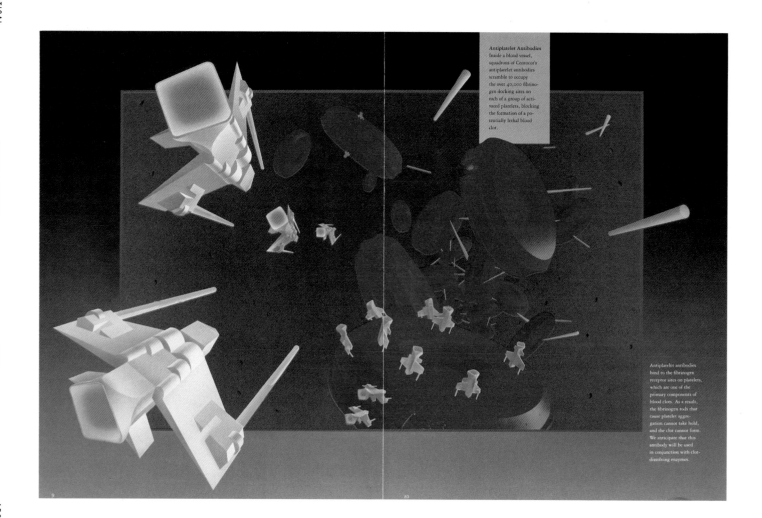

Diagrammatic illustration for Centocor's annual report. It shows how this biopharmaceutical company's products fight off infection.
セントコア社のアニュアルリポートより、同社の医薬品が感染と戦う様子を描いているイラストレーション。

STATISTICAL
TABLES & GRAPHS

CHARTS & SCORES

MAPS

ARCHITECTURAL
PLANS & DRAWINGS

INSTRUCTIONAL DIAGRAMS
FOR PRODUCTS

SCIENTIFIC
ILLUSTRATIONS

ARCO
USA 1991
CD:Ron Jefferies
D:Scott Lambert
P:Keith Wood
I:Hank Fisher
DF:The Jefferies Association

ARCO's reformulation of gasolines adds the oxygenate methyl tertiary butyl ether (MTBE) while reducing the content of benzene (by more than 50 percent), aromatics and butane which causes evaporative emissions.

While EC-1 replaced leaded fuel for older cars and trucks, ARCO's EC-Premium is designed to meet the needs of late-model high-performance engines. These changes were achieved without increased cost to the consumer.

George H. Babikian
President
ARCO Products Co.

"ARCO is committed to finding realistic clean air solutions. Our mission is to put clean-burning gasolines in all cars that are on the road today. There are 185 million registered vehicles on U.S. roads today that cannot run on most of the alternative fuels being discussed. We believe that reformulated gasoline is the best option for reducing vehicular emissions."

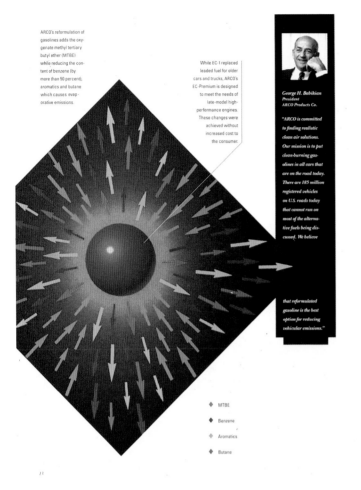

◆ MTBE
◆ Benzene
◆ Aromatics
◆ Butane

ARCO Chemical has more than 20 years' experience with oxygenated fuels that have environmental and performance benefits. In the last 10 years, the Company has become the world's leading producer of MTBE.

MTBE, a simple molecular compound comprising oxygen, carbon and hydrogen, has several unique qualities. It boosts octane in unleaded gasoline and reduces automotive emissions that contribute to smog and ozone pollution.

Alan R. Hirsig
President and Chief
Executive Officer
ARCO Chemical Co.

"ARCO Chemical anticipates that demand for MTBE will grow substantially worldwide as the result of the U.S. Clean Air Act Amendments, which have created a fast-growing market for reformulated gasolines, and the growth of unleaded fuels in Europe. We currently have production capability for MTBE in the U.S., the Netherlands and France, and we expect to expand capacity where we have a technological or cost advantage."

◆ Oxygen
◆ Hydrogen
◆ Carbon

Diagram showing the chemical make-up of clean burning ECI gasoline. The colored arrows represent different chemicals.
Diagram showing the molecular structure of MTBE, an additive which boosts the octane of unleaded gasoline and reduces automotive emissions. From an Arco annual report.
アルコ社のアニュアルリポートより、クリーンに燃焼するECIガソリンの科学的構成を表したイラストレーション。色別の矢印はそれぞれ異なった化学薬品を示している。
無鉛ガソリンのオクタン価を上げ、自動車排出物を減らすことができる添加剤MTBEの分子構造図。

GAKKEN

JAPAN 1982
CD:Yuji Yamanaka
I:Ukei Tomori

STATISTICAL
TABLES & GRAPHS

CHARTS & SCORES

MAPS

ARCHITECTURAL
PLANS & DRAWINGS

INSTRUCTIONAL DIAGRAMS
FOR PRODUCTS

SCIENTIFIC
ILLUSTRATIONS

科学雑誌や映画のパンフレットに掲載された南極大陸パノラマ。

Panoramic diagram of the Antarctic. From a science magazine and a program for a movie.
科学雑誌や映画のパンフレットに掲載された南極大陸パノラマ。

STATISTICAL
TABLES & GRAPHS

CHARTS & SCORES

MAPS

ARCHITECTURAL
PLANS & DRAWINGS

INSTRUCTIONAL DIAGRAMS
FOR PRODUCTS

SCIENTIFIC
ILLUSTRATIONS

BLUE MOON STUDIO INC.

JAPAN 1992

AD,D:Masato Okazaki

I:Takatoshi Oki

Illustration comparing the size of humans and dinosaurs.

人間と恐竜の大きさを比較したイラストレーション。

STATISTICAL
TABLES & GRAPHS

CHARTS & SCORES

MAPS

ARCHITECTURAL
PLANS & DRAWINGS

INSTRUCTIONAL DIAGRAMS
FOR PRODUCTS

SCIENTIFIC
ILLUSTRATIONS

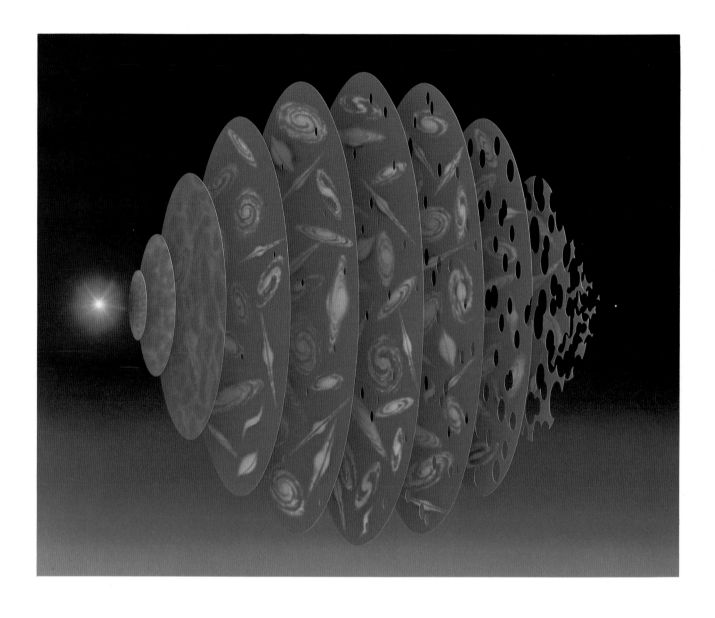

科学雑誌「ニュートン別冊/ブラックホール宇宙」より、宇宙はビックバン特異点に始まりビッククランチ特異点に終わるという"特異点定理"のイラストレーション。

Illustration of the "singular state" theory which postulates that the Universe started at the Big Bang singular state and will end at the Big Crunch singular state.
From a special edition of the scientific magazine "Newton".
科学雑誌「ニュートン別冊/ブラックホール宇宙」より、宇宙はビックバン特異点に始まりビッククランチ特異点に終わるという"特異点定理"のイラストレーション。

STATISTICAL
TABLES & GRAPHS

CHARTS & SCORES

MAPS

ARCHITECTURAL
PLANS & DRAWINGS

INSTRUCTIONAL DIAGRAMS
FOR PRODUCTS

SCIENTIFIC
ILLUSTRATIONS

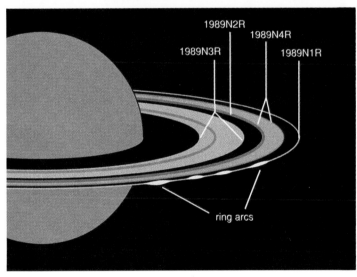

Diagrams of the ring systems of Jupiter, Uranus, Neptune and Saturn. Each planetary system has a unique complement of rings,
varying in width, height and density as well as the size and composition of its particles. From American Scientist magazine.
「アメリカン・サイエンティストマガジン」より、木星・天王星・海王星・土星の輪を表したダイアグラム。各惑星には幅・高さ・密度さらには大きさ・組成の異なった粒子からなる独特の輪がある。

STATISTICAL TABLES & GRAPHS

CHARTS & SCORES

MAPS

ARCHITECTURAL PLANS & DRAWINGS

INSTRUCTIONAL DIAGRAMS FOR PRODUCTS

SCIENTIFIC ILLUSTRATIONS

NORCEN ENERGY RESOURCES
USA 1991
AD:Kit Hinrichs
D:Piper Murakami
I:Helene Moore
DF:Pentagram Design Ltd.

GREAT CORAL REEFS
USA 1992
AD:Jeff Batzli
D:Susan Livingston
I:Scott MacNeill
DF:Micheal Friedman Publishing Group

珊瑚礁の姿を海底から海面上まで描き、様々な特長を解説したイラストレーション。

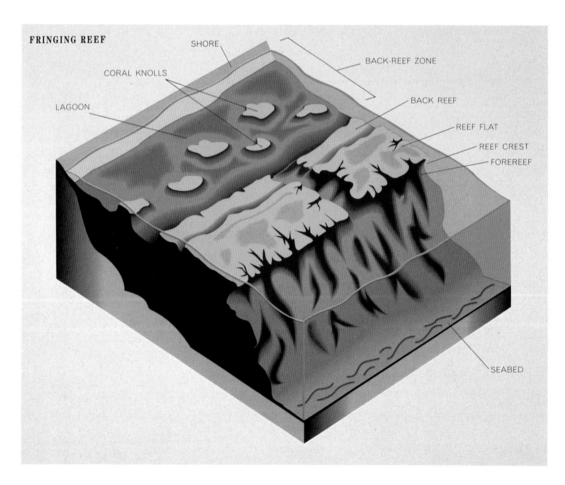

Cross-sectional view of sea-bed soil substrata showing layers rich in gas,
oil and indicating the earthquake factor. From a Norcen Energy Resources annual report.
ノーセン・エナジー・リゾース社のアニュアルリポートより、地震分析の様子、
及び海底や地底深くに存在するガス・オイルの地層等を表す地層断面図。

Illustration showing what a coral reef looks like, from its base,
to above the water line and pointing out its different features.
珊瑚礁の姿を海底から海面上まで描き、様々な特長を解説したイラストレーション。

INDEX

INDEX

DIAGRAM GRAPHICS

AD INTERNATIONAL INC. 194

ALAN KIKUCHI 155, 189

AMERICAN SCIENTIST 119, 215

ANDY MARTIN 115

AXIS INCORPORATED 128

BAY GRAPHICS DESIGN INC. 87

BBC TELEVISION, NEWS & CURRENT AFFAIRS GRAPHIC DESIGN DEPARTMENT 60, 61, 151

BBV 63

BEAUCHAMP GROUP 25, 53

BELK MIGNOGNA ASSOC. 19, 84, 148

BESSER JOSEPH PARTNERS 76, 86

BILL FINEWOOD 208

BLUE MOON STUDIO INC. 190, 213

CARL SELTZER DESIGN OFFICE 23, 24, 33, 34, 36, 39, 196

COMMUNICATION BY DESIGN 62, 152, 174

COMMUNITY & COMMUNICATION CO., LTD. 44, 45, 65, 138

COOK AND SHANOSKY ASSOCIATES, INC. 38, 40

COREY MCPHERSON NASH 29, 32, 33

CS COOPSTUDIO 137

EARL GEE DESIGN 54, 90

DENTSU INC. 68

ECO-ID. 169, 188

EDITRICE PROGETTI 183

ESKIND WADDELL 41, 85, 130

FORBES MAGAZINE 31

FORSYTHE DESIGN 101

FRANK FASANO 201

GAN HOSOYA/LIGHT PUBLICITY LTD. 71

GRAPHIC COMMUNICATION CONCEPTS 175

GRAPHIC COMMUNICATION LTD. 56

GRUNDY + NORTHEDGE 52, 69, 70, 109, 110,114

HENRY DREYFUSS ASSOCIATES 108

HIDEO MIZOKAWA 198

HITACHI SALES CORPORATION 193

HORNALL ANDERSON DESIGN WORKS 51, 55, 75, 78, 111, 140, 156

IBI, INC. 95

ICHIRO HIGASHIIZUMI 91, 100, 129

INC DESIGN 18

JACK HOUGH ASSOCIATES 12, 13, 23

JERDE PARTNERSHIP 163

JOHN DAUGHERTY 206, 207

JONES MEDINGER KINDSCHI BUSHKO 64, 82

KAN TAI-KEUNG DESIGN & ASSOCIATES LTD. 20, 35

KANO DESIGN GROUP INC. 11, 14, 16, 22, 57, 177

KATZ DESIGN GROUP 31, 42, 124, 125, 210

KIHARU TSUGE 102

KLAUS HERDEG 164

KYOIKUSHA, LTD. 214

LINTAS MARKETING COMMUNICATIONS. INC, 22

LOUIS NELSON ASSOCIATES 168

MACNEILL & MACINTOSH 112, 148, 216

MADDISON/MOORE GRAPHICS 30, 70, 132, 133

MATT ZANG 149

MITSUNOBU MURAKAMI 106

MORISHITA CO., LTD. 129

NATIONAL GEOGRAPHIC SOCIETY 139

NIGEL HOLMES 72, 149, 150

NORIAKI KANEKO 204

OUT SIDE DIRECTORS CO., LTD. 100

P3 ART AND ENVIRONMENT 160

PENCIL CORPORATE ART 58, 180

PENTAGRAM DESIGN LTD. (LONDON) 26, 37, 53, 80, 81, 83, 92, 93, 120, 123, 127, 156, 201

PENTAGRAM DESIGN LTD. (SAN FRANCISCO) 142, 154, 176, 178, 216

PETER BRADFORD 96, 97, 126, 202, 203

PIONEER ELECTRIC CORPORATION 191

POWER HOUSE MUSEUM 172, 173

PROFESSIONAL MARKETING SERVICES 59

PLUS DESIGN INC. 103

R.D.E. RICERCHE DESIGN EDITRICE S.R.L. 192

RAY ENGLE & ASSOCIATES 32, 43, 98, 116, 146

RAYMOND BENNETT DESGIN 43

RICHARD GAGE 50

ROBERT P. GERSIN ASSOCIATES INC. 99, 125

SABIN DESIGN 113, 135

SARU BRUNEI CO., LTD. 94, 131

SIR NORMAN FOSTER & PARTNERS 166

SONOE TAKIGAMI 67, 107

SONY CORPORATION 191

STEPHEN WOLF 158

STEVEN GUARNACCIA'S STUDIO 135, 137

STUDIO WORKS 136, 153

T.Y.D. INC. 170

TATHAM PEARCE LIMITED 35, 48, 111, 134, 135

TETSUYA OHTA 21, 28, 46, 47, 89, 159

THE GRAPHIC EXPRESSION, INC. 27, 66, 115, 116, 140, 184, 186, 209

THE JEFFERIES ASSOCIATION 43, 79, 118, 144, 145, 211

THE PRESENTATION COMPANY 60, 61, 151

UKEI TOMORI 212

UNA 88

WORKSHOP INC. 165

YUKIMASA MATSUDA 99, 104, 105

INDEX

DIAGRAM GRAPHICS

DIAGRAM COLLECTION

ART DIRECTOR
Kazuo Abe

JACKET DESIGNER
Yutaka Ichimura

DESIGNERS
Yutaka Ichimura
Kimiko Ishiwatari
Shinji Ikenoue

EDITORS
Yuko Yoshio
Tsutomu Hirata

EDITORIAL MANAGER
Masato Ieshiro

PHOTOGRAPHER
Shoichi Sato (Photo Studio Techne)

ENGLISH TRANSLATOR & ADVISER
Write Away Co., Ltd.

COORDINATORS
Roland Gebhardt Design (New York)
Sarah Phillips (London)

PUBLISHER
Shingo Miyoshi

EDITORIAL CONSULTANT
Fumihiko Nishioka

1997年6月23日初版第1刷発行

発行所　ピエ・ブックス
〒170 東京都豊島区駒込4-14-6-301
TEL: 03-3940-8302 FAX: 03-3576-7361
e-mail: piebooks@bekkoame.or.jp

製版　(株)飛来社
印刷・製本　(株)サンニチ印刷

CORPORATE IMAGE DESIGN
世界の業種別CI・ロゴマーク
Pages: 336 (272 in Color)　¥16,000
An effective logo is the key to brand or company recognition. This sourcebook of total CI design introduces pieces created for a wide range of businesses - from boutiques to multinationals - and features hundreds of design concepts and applications.

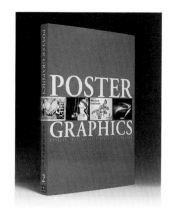

POSTER GRAPHICS Vol. 2
好評！業種別世界のポスター集大成、第2弾
Pages: 256 (192 in Color)　¥17,000
700 posters from the top creators in Japan and abroad are showcased in this book - classified by business. This invaluable reference makes it easy to compare design trends among various industries and corporations.

BROCHURE & PAMPHLET COLLECTION Vol. 4
好評！業種別カタログ・コレクション、第4弾
Pages: 224 (Full Color)　¥16,000
The fourth volume in our popular "Brochure & Pamphlet" series. Twelve types of businesses are represented through artwork that really sells. This book conveys a sense of what's happening right now in the catalog design scene. A must for all creators.

BROCHURE DESIGN FORUM Vol. 2
世界の最新カタログ・コレクション
Pages: 224 (176 in Color)　¥16,000
A special edition of our "Brochure & Pamphlet Collection" featuring 250 choice pieces that represent 70 types of businesses and are classified by business for handy reference. A compendium of the design scene at a glance.

A CATALOGUE AND PAMPHLET COLLECTION
業種別商品カタログ特集／ソフトカバー
Pages: 224 (Full Color)　¥3,800
A collection of the world's most outstanding brochures, catalogs and leaflets classified by industry such as fashion, restaurants, music, interiors and sports goods. Presenting each piece in detail from cover to inside. This title is an indispensable sourcebook for all graphic designers and CI professionals.

COMPANY BROCHURE COLLECTION
業種別（会社・学校・施設）案内グラフィックス
Pages: 224 (192 in Color)　¥16,000
A rare selection of brochures and catalogs ranging from admission manuals for colleges and universities, to amusement facility and hotel guidebooks, to corporate and organization profiles. The entries are classified by industry for easy reference.

COMPANY BROCHURE COLLECTION Vol. 2
業種別会社案内グラフィックス　第2弾！
Pages: 224 (Full Color)　¥16,000
Showing imaginative layouts that present information clearly in limited space, and design that effectively enhances corporate identity, this volume will prove to be an essential source book for graphic design work of the future.

CORPORATE PROFILE GRAPHICS
世界の会社案内グラフィックス
Pages: 224 (Full Color)　¥16,000
A new version of our popular "Brochure and Pamphlet Collection" series featuring 200 carefully selected catalogs from around the world. A substantial variety of school brochures, company profiles and facility information is offered.

CREATIVE FLYER GRAPHICS Vol. 2
世界のフライヤーデザイン傑作選
Pages: 224 (Full Color)　¥16,000
A pack of some 600 flyers and leaflets incorporating information from a variety of events including exhibitions, movies, plays, concerts, live entertainment and club events, as well as foods, cosmetics, electrical merchandise and travel packages.

EVENT FLYER GRAPHICS
世界のイベントフライヤー・コレクション
Pages: 224 (Full Color)　¥16,000
Here's a special selection zooming in on flyers promoting events. This upbeat selection covers wide-ranging music events, as well as movies, exhibitions and the performing arts.

ADVERTISING FLYER GRAPHICS
衣・食・住・遊の商品チラシ特集
Pages: 224 (Full Color)　¥16,000
The eye-catching flyers selected for this new collection represent a broad spectrum of businesses, and are presented in a loose classification covering four essential areas of modern lifestyles: fashion, dining, home and leisure.

CALENDAR GRAPHICS Vol. 2
好評カレンダー・デザイン集の決定版、第2弾
Pages: 224 (192 in Color)　¥16,000
The second volume of our popular "Calendar Graphics" features designs from about 250 1994 and 1995 calendars from around the world. A rare collection including those on the market as well as exclusive corporate PR calendars.

DIAGRAM GRAPHICS Vol. 2
世界のダイアグラム・デザインの集大成
Pages: 224 (192 in Color)　￥16,000
The unsurpassed second volume in our "Diagram Graphics" series is now complete, thanks to cooperation from artists around the world. It features graphs, charts and maps created for various media.

NEW TYPO GRAPHICS
世界の最新タイポグラフィ・コレクション
Pages: 224 (192 in Color)　￥16,000
Uncompromising in its approach to typographic design, this collection includes 350 samples of only the very finest works available. This special collection is a compendium of all that is exciting along the leading edge of typographic creativity today.

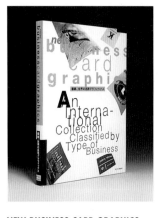

1, 2 & 3 COLOR GRAPHICS
1・2・3 色グラフィックス
Pages: 208 (Full Color)　￥16,000
Featured here are outstanding graphics in limited colors. See about 300 samples of 1,2 & 3-color artwork that are so expressive they often surpass the impact of full four-color reproductions. This is a very important book that will expand the possibilities of your design work in the future.

1, 2 & 3 COLOR GRAPHICS Vol. 2
1・2・3 色グラフィックス、第 2 弾
Pages: 224 (Full Color)　￥16,000
Even more ambitious in scale than the first volume, this second collection of graphics displays the unique talents of graphic designers who work with limited colors. An essential reference guide to effective, low-cost designing.

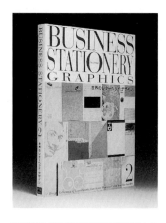

BUSINESS STATIONERY GRAPHICS Vol. 2
世界のレターヘッド・コレクション、第2弾
Pages: 224 (176 in Color)　￥16,000
The second volume in our popular "Business Stationery Graphics" series. This publication focuses on letterheads, envelopes and business cards, all classified by business. Our collection will serve artists and business people well.

BUSINESS CARD GRAPHICS Vol. 1 / Soft Jacket
世界の名刺コレクション／ソフトカバー
Pages: 224 (160 in Color)　￥3,800
First impressions of an individual or company are often shaped by their business cards. The 1,200 corporate and personal-use business cards shown here illustrate the design strategies of 500 top Japanese, American and European designers. PIE's most popular book.

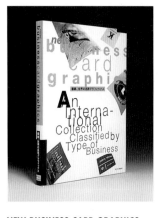

NEW BUSINESS CARD GRAPHICS
最新版！ビジネスカード グラフィックス
Pages: 224(Full Color)　￥16,000
A selection of 900 samples representing the works of top designers worldwide. Covering the broadest spectrum of business categories, this selection of the world's best business cards ranges from the trendiest to the most classy and includes highly original examples along the way.

BUSINESS PUBLICATION GRAPHICS
業種別企業ＰＲ誌・フリーペーパーの集大成！
Pages: 224 (Full Color)　￥16,000
This comprehensive graphic book introduces business publications created for a variety of business needs, including promotions from boutiques and department stores, exclusive clubs, local communities and company newsletters.

POSTCARD GRAPHICS Vol. 4
世界の業種別ポストカード・コレクション
Pages: 224 (192 in Color)　￥16,000
Our popular "Postcard Graphics" series has been revamped for "Postcard Graphics Vol. 4." This first volume of the new version showcases approximately 1,000 pieces ranging from direct mailers to private greeting cards, selected from the best around the world.

POSTCARD COLLECTION Vol. 2
ポストカードコレクション／ソフトカバー
Pages: 230 (Full Color)　￥3,800
Welcome to the colorful world of postcards with 1200 postcards created by artists from all over the world classified according to the business of the client.

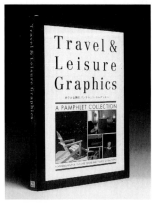

TRAVEL & LEISURE GRAPHICS
ホテル＆旅行 案内 グラフィックス
Pages: 224 (Full Color)　￥16,000
A giant collection of some 400 pamphlets, posters and direct mailings exclusively delivered for hotels, inns, resort tours and amusement facilities.

SPECIAL EVENT GRAPHICS
世界のイベント・グラフィックス
Pages: 224 (192 in Color)　￥16,000
A showcase for event graphics, introducing leaflets for exhibitions, fashion shows, all sorts of sales promotional campaigns, posters, premiums and actual installation scenes from events around the world. An invaluable and inspirational resource book, unique in the world of graphic publishing.

3-D GRAPHICS
3Dグラフィックスの大百科
Pages: 224 (192 in Color) ￥16,000
350 works that demonstrate some of the finest examples of 3-D graphic methods, including DMs, catalogs, posters, POPs and more. The volume is a virtual encyclopedia of 3-D graphics.

PROMOTIONAL GREETING CARDS
ADVERTISING GREETING CARDS Vol. 4
(English Title)
厳選された世界の案内状＆DM
Pages: 224 (Full Color) ￥16,000
A total of 500 examples of cards from designers around the world. A whole spectrum of stylish and inspirational cards, are classified by function for easy reference.

DIRECT MAIL GRAPHICS Vol. 1
衣・食・住のセールスDM特集
Pages: 224 (Full Color) ￥16,000
The long-awaited design collection featuring direct mailers with outstanding sales impact and quality design. 350 of the best pieces, classified into 100 business categories.
A veritable textbook of current direct-marketing design.

DIRECT MAIL GRAPHICS Vol. 2
好評！衣・食・住のセールスDM特集！第2弾
Pages: 224 (Full Color) ￥16,000
The second volume in our extremely popular "Direct Mail Graphics" series features a whole range of direct mailers for various purposes; from commercial announcements to seasonal greetings and are also classified by industry.

T-SHIRT GRAPHICS / Soft Jacket
世界のTシャツ・コレクション / ソフトカバー
Pages: 224 (192 in Color) ￥3,800
This stunning showcase publication features about 700 T-shirts collected from the major international design centers. Includes various promotional shirts and fabulous designs from the fashion world and sporting-goods manufacturers as well. This eagerly awaited publication has arrived at just the right time.

T-SHIRT PRINT DESIGNS & LOGOS
世界のTシャツ・プリント デザイン＆ロゴ
Pages: 224 (192 in Color) ￥16,000
Second volume of our popular "T-shirt Graphics" series. In this publication, 800 designs for T-shirt graphics, including many trademarks and logotypes are showcased. The world's top designers in the field are featured.

The Paris Collections / INVITATION CARDS
パリ・コレクションの招待状グラフィックス
Pages: 176 (Full Color) ￥13,800
This book features 400 announcements for and invitations to the Paris Collections, produced by the world's top names in fashion over the past 10 years. A treasure trove of ideas and pure fun to browse through.

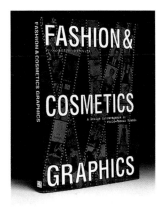

FASHION & COSMETICS GRAPHICS
ファッション＆コスメティック・グラフィックス
Pages: 208 (Full Color) ￥16,000
A collection of promotional graphics from around the world produced for apparel, accessory and cosmetic brands at the avant-garde of the fashion industry. 40 brands featured in this book point the way toward future trends in advertising.

SPORTS GRAPHICS / Soft Jacket
世界のスポーツグッズ・コレクション / ソフトカバー
Pages: 224 (192 in Color) ￥3,800
A collection of 1,000 bold sporting-goods graphic works from all over the world. A wide variety of goods are shown, including uniforms, bags, shoes and other gear. Covers all sorts of sports: basketball, skiing, surfing and many, many more.

LABELS AND TAGS COLLECTION Vol. 1 / Soft Jaket
ラベル＆タグ・コレクション / ソフトカバー
Pages: 224 (192 in Color) ￥3,800
Nowhere is brand recognition more important than in Japan. Here is a collection of 1,600 labels and tags from Japan's 450 top fashion names with page after page of women's and men's clothing and sportswear designs.

INSIGNIA COLLECTION
ワッペン＆エンブレム・コレクション／ソフトカバー
Pages: 224 (Full Color) ￥3,800
Over 3000 designs were scrutinized for this collection of 1000 outstanding emblems and embroidered motifs that are visually exciting, make innovative use of materials and compliment the fashions with which they are worn.

CD JACKET COLLECTION
世界のCDジャケット・コレクション／ソフトカバー
Pages: 224 (192 in Color) ￥3,800
Featuring 700 of the world's most imaginative CD and LP covers from all musical genres, this is a must-have book for all design and music professionals.

TYPO-DIRECTION IN JAPAN Vol. 6
年鑑 日本のタイポディレクション '94-'95
Pages: 250 (Full Color) ¥17,000
This book features the finest work from the international competition of graphic design in Japan. The sixth volume of our popular yearbook series is edited by the TOKYO TYPE DIRECTORS CLUB with the participation of master designers worldwide.

THE TOKYO TYPEDIRECTORS CLUB ANNUAL 1995-96
TDC 年鑑95-96
Pages: 250 (Full Color) ¥17,000
A follow-up publication to Japan's only international graphic design competition. Featuring 650 typographic artworks selected by THE TOKYO TYPEDIRECTORS CLUB, this book provides a window on the latest typographic design concepts worldwide.

The Production Index ARTIFILE Vol. 4
活躍中！広告プロダクション年鑑、第4弾
Pages: 224 (Full Color) ¥12,500
The fourth volume in our "Production Index Artifile" series features vigorously selected yearly artworks from 107 outstanding production companies and artists in Japan. An invaluable source book of the current design forefronts portraying their policies and backgrounds.

The Production Index ARTIFILE Vol.5
最新版プロダクション・クリエーター年鑑
Pages: 224(Full Color) ¥12,500
ARTIFILE 5 features artwork from a total of 100 top Japanese production companies and designers, along with company data and messages from the creators. An invaluable information source for anyone who needs to keep up with the latest developments in the graphic scene.

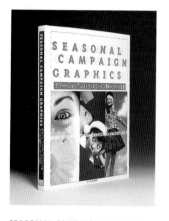

SEASONAL CAMPAIGN GRAPHICS
デパート・ショップのキャンペーン広告特集
Pages: 224 (Full Color) ¥16,000
A spirited collection of quality graphics for sales campaigns planned around the four seasons and Christmas, St. Valentines Day and the Japanese gift-giving seasons, as well as for store openings, anniversaries, and similar events.

SHOPPING BAG GRAPHICS
世界の最新ショッピング・バッグデザイン集
Pages: 224 (Full Color) ¥16,000
Over 500 samples of the latest and best of the world's shopping bag design from a wide selection of retail businesses! This volume features a selection of shopping bags originating in Tokyo, NY, LA, London, Paris, Milan and other major cities worldwide, and presented here in a useful business classification.

CARTOON CHARACTER COLLECTION
5500種のキャラクターデザイン大百科
Pages: 480 (B&W) ¥9,800
A total of 5,500 cartoons and illustrations from some of the most successful illustrations in the industry have been carefully selected for this giant, new collection. The illustrations included are classified by animals, figures, vehicles, etc, for easy reference.

カタログ・新刊のご案内について
総合カタログ、新刊案内をご希望の方は、はさみ込みのアンケートはがきを
ご返送いただくか、90円切手同封の上、ピエ・ブックス宛お申し込み下さい。

CATALOGUES ET INFORMATIONS SUR LES NOUVELLES PUBLICATIONS
Si vous désirez recevoir un exemplaire gratuit de notre catalogue général ou des détails sur vos nouvelles publications, veuillez compléter la carte réponse incluse et nous la retourner par courrierou par fax.

CATALOGS and INFORMATION ON NEW PUBLICATIONS
If you would like to receive a free copy of our general catalog or details of our new publications, please fill out the enclosed postcard and return it to us by mail or fax.

CATALOGE und INFORMATIONEN ÜBER NEUE TITLE
Wenn Sie unseren Gesamtkatalog oder Detailinformationen über unsere neuen Titel wünschen, fullen Sie bitte die beigefügte Postkarte aus und schicken Sie sie uns per Post oder Fax.

ピエ・ブックス
〒170 東京都豊島区駒込 4-14-6-301
TEL: 03-3940-8302 FAX: 03-3576-7361

P·I·E BOOKS
#301, 4-14-6, Komagome, Toshima-ku, Tokyo 170 JAPAN
TEL: 813-3940-8302 FAX: 813-3576-7361